Lawyer Like AN ATHLETE

How to Up Your Game at Work and in Life

AMY WOOD

AMERICAN BAR ASSOCIATION
Solo, Small Firm and General Practice Division

Cover design by Mary Anne Kulchawik/ABA Design

Printed in the United States of America.

28 27 26 25 24   5 4 3 2 1

Library of Congress Cataloging-in-Publication Data

Names: Wood, Amy, author. | American Bar Association. Section of Litigation, issuing body.
Title: Lawyer like an athlete : how to up your game at work and in life / author, Amy Wood, Psy.D.
Description: 1st edition. | Chicago : American Bar Association, Section litigation, 2024. | Includes index. | Summary: "I have observed this conundrum play out with disturbing regularity at different stages of lawyers' careers. Newer lawyers often sacrificed much to earn top grades, high class rank, and prestigious positions on law review journals so that they could land a high-paying job with a large private law firm. After attaining their goal of a plum position, a sizeable number start looking for a different job within the first, second, or third year of practice because they find the work, the stress, and the lifestyle both unmanageable and unsustainable. Other attorneys sail through those first few years with seeming ease, but later run into serious headwinds in their later associate years as they are trying to develop their own practice, make partner, contribute pro bono and/or community service hours, often with young children at home. Sadly, many of these still early-career attorneys leave private practice for other legal jobs they hope will be less stressful, and some even give up on their dream of practicing law entirely. The reason is the same-they find the work, the stress, and the lifestyle unmanageable and unsustainable"-- Provided by publisher.
Identifiers: LCCN 2024013258 (print) | LCCN 2024013259 (ebook) | ISBN 9781639054855 (paperback) | ISBN 9781639054862 (epub)
Subjects: LCSH: Practice of law--United States. | Law--Vocational guidance--United States. | Lawyers--United States.
Classification: LCC KF300 .W66 2024 (print) | LCC KF300 (ebook) | DDC 340.023/73--dc23/eng/20240402
LC record available at https://lccn.loc.gov/2024013258
LC ebook record available at https://lccn.loc.gov/2024013259

ISBN 978-1-63905-485-5

Discounts are available for books ordered in bulk. Special consideration is given to state bars, CLE programs, and other bar-related organizations. Inquire at Book Publishing, ABA Publishing, American Bar Association, 321 N. Clark Street, Chicago, Illinois 60654-7598.

www.shopABA.org

ADVANCE PRAISE FOR *LAWYER LIKE AN ATHLETE*

"Just like her CLE presentations, Dr. Wood's book is kind, authentic, meaningful, and delivered in a manner that is both entertaining and enlightening. Every Lawyer Assistance Program should have it on hand for their clients."

–Mike Larson, Coordinator, Montana Lawyer Assistance Program

"*Lawyer Like an Athlete* is an indispensable guide to solving the attorney stress problem. Similar to her no-nonsense CLE programs, Dr. Wood's book surpasses standard self-help advice with attorney-specific strategies that are manageable, sustainable, and truly constructive."

–Linda Morin-Pasco, Continuing Legal Education Director, Maine State Bar

"With *Lawyer Like an Athlete*, Dr. Wood provides practical tips for making small, attainable changes that can lead to large-scale results. Her exercises in self-inventory teach you how to confront and scale back habits that don't serve you and maximize ones that do. Her approach juxtaposing athlete training and performance onto lawyering is unique and effective."

–Erika S. Kahill, Board Member, Anchorage Association of Women Lawyers

"As an attorney turned mindfulness expert to attorneys, I know how vulnerable lawyers are to losing balance professionally and personally. I recommend *Lawyer Like an Athlete* as an accessible, pragmatic training manual for tackling the tough challenges of practicing law in a more grounded, skillful, and successful way."

—Terry Fralich, LCPC, JD, author of The Five Core Skills of Mindfulness *and* Cultivating Lasting Happiness: A 7-Step Guide to Mindfulness

"*Lawyer Like an Athlete* takes direct aim at the high rates of toxic stress, anxiety, and depression that plague the legal profession. Smart, practical, and wise, this book should be on every lawyer's must-read list."

—Daniel T. Lukasik, Esq., Judicial Wellness Coordinator for the NYS Office of Court Administration; Professor of Law, University of Buffalo School of Law; and creator of the website Lawyerswithdepression.com

"*Lawyer Like an Athlete* provides an original solution to the problem that plagues most attorneys: "no time" for a healthy work/life symmetry. Dr. Wood's workbook approach invites lawyers to improve how they work and live step by manageable step and includes many motivating examples of attorneys who have benefitted from her knowledge and advice. I highly recommend *Lawyer Like an Athlete* to everyone—attorneys and non-attorneys alike—wanting to thrive amid the very real and unrelenting stress of the legal world."

—Lynn Whittingham, CLE Coordinator, Alaska Bar Association

"Drawing from the author's expertise as a psychologist and her passion for empowering high achievers, *Lawyer Like an Athlete* addresses lawyer-specific peak performance challenges with innovative solutions inspired by professional sports. The book's structured approach as a sensible training manual invites readers to progress at their own pace, allowing them to apply the strategies and exercises in a manner that resonates with their individual demands and goals. Whether you are a seasoned attorney or a recent law school graduate, this relatable and empowering book is a must-have pathway to unparalleled fulfillment and excellence in the legal profession."

—Esther Uria LaBovick, Esq.; Shareholder and Chief Legal Officer, LaBovick Law Group

"*Lawyer Like an Athlete* is a must-read for any attorney, or aspiring attorney, who struggles with burnout, stress, or work-life balance. Through real stories and practical exercises, Dr. Amy Wood breaks down the myth that you cannot be a successful lawyer and have a fulfilling life. In fact, she shows that being a successful attorney with a fulfilling life doesn't have to be as difficult as we make it out to be. This book is essential for attorneys who want an easier way."

—Katie Day Winchenbach, Program Director, Ms. JD

"Dr. Wood has a great grasp on what lawyers are dealing with today. With an interactive approach and examples from real attorneys, this book helps lawyers to learn and understand why we think, feel, and act in ways that do not always serve us. The book allows for written reflection and encourages growth with a healthy dose of much-needed self-compassion."

—Kristin Murray-James, Esq., Executive Director, Maine Assistance Program for Lawyers and Judges

CONTENTS

AUTHOR'S NOTE

The instructions and advice in *Lawyer Like an Athlete* are not intended as a substitute for psychotherapy or coaching. I disclaim any responsibility or liability resulting from actions advocated or discussed in this book.

In the interest of preserving confidentiality, the clients and circumstances portrayed in this book are composite in nature. Any resemblance of a composite character to an actual person is entirely coincidental.

FOREWORD

Before I became the CEO of Maine's largest law firm, I both practiced law and led attorney recruiting and retention for my firm. With more than two decades of law firm experience under my belt, I've learned two realities are true simultaneously:

One: many attorneys enter the field of law to solve the world's most complex and exciting legal problems, pursue justice, and/or help make the world a better place—and many succeed. This is the power of law: knowing how the system works, and how advocacy can advance lawful goals, right wrongs, and progress change.

Two: while the law is a lofty and learned profession, it is also an extraordinarily exacting one that exerts a heavy toll on lawyers and leaves many feeling disillusioned, disappointed, and at sea with their careers. Many also become profoundly unhealthy as they adopt a tunnel-vision mindset to ignore the self—mental, physical, and emotional wellness—in pursuit of professional excellence.

I have observed this conundrum play out with disturbing regularity at different stages of lawyers' careers. Newer lawyers often sacrificed much to earn top grades, high class rank, and prestigious positions at law review journals so that they could land a high-paying job with a large private law firm. After attaining their goal of a plum position, a sizeable number start looking for a different job within the first, second, or third year of practice because they find the work, the stress, and the lifestyle both unmanageable and unsustainable. Other attorneys sail through those first few years with seeming ease but later run into serious headwinds in their later associate years as they are trying to develop their own practice or make partner, and contribute pro bono and/or community service hours, often with young children at home. Sadly, many of these still early-career attorneys leave private practice for other legal jobs they hope will be less stressful, and some even give up on their dream of practicing law entirely. The reason is the same—they find the work, the stress, and the lifestyle unmanageable and unsustainable.

A final observable pattern is from the more senior lawyer, who pushed through the heavy demands of private practice so hard and for so long and did attain that prestigious position of partner. Something eventually breaks—physically, mentally, relationally—or they experience complete burnout, and their tank runs dry.

I had been observing these patterns for many years when, in 2016, I read the American Bar Association's damning study of 13,000 practicing lawyers, which documented alarmingly high rates of substance abuse, chronic stress, poor mental health, and suicide among them. By January 2020, when I became my firm's CEO, I knew that we needed to attend to the mental health and well-being of lawyers—not just in my firm but within the profession as a whole.

And then the global COVID-19 pandemic hit two months into my tenure. That is when I called Dr. Amy Wood.

I had met Dr. Wood a few years earlier over coffee at a local coffee shop in Portland, Maine. I was interested to learn that she is a doctorate-level clinical psychologist who specializes in attorney wellness and provides both group training programs and individualized coaching to lawyers across the country. Shortly thereafter, we hired Dr. Wood to coach one of our partners who was struggling to manage and keep up with their busy practice and busy life. I observed from the sidelines how that attorney embraced and worked through Dr. Wood's positive, step-by-step approach, and in a reasonably short period of time, they had turned things around and were thriving again at work and home.

Since the onset of the pandemic, Dr. Wood has been my go-to resource for mental health and well-being training and coaching for our firm. I have learned that Dr. Wood has a deep understanding of the intense stress that private practice lawyers are under in today's hyperconnected and always-on world. Conducting her own unique research, Dr. Wood found attorney stress to be so far outside the norm of what other stressed professionals experience that she defines it as "attorney outlier stress." Importantly, she also has developed a deep reservoir of strategies and techniques to help attorneys recapture control over their careers in a way that fosters better mental health and well-being and more positive relationships inside and outside of the office.

Now, in *Lawyer Like an Athlete,* Dr. Wood combines her 20-plus years of experience helping hundreds of lawyers thrive at work with observations, training tips, and customized game plans. She shares with us a holistic, sensible, and structured training manual to help lawyers achieve peak performance at home and work by taking care of mind, body, and spirit. The biggest insight? Dr. Wood borrows from the world of elite athletics.

Inspired by watching Serena Williams play tennis on television, Dr. Wood made the connection that elite athletes and attorneys are in a league of their own concerning the elevated pressure and expectations they face in fields demanding prolonged and repeated peak performance, requiring intense stamina, uncommon resilience, and rigor. Dr. Wood reminds us repeatedly throughout her book that neither athletes nor attorneys can "win" at the expense of their mental health and well-being.

Structured as a positive and action-oriented training program designed to boost performance rather than a self-help primer, *Lawyer Like an Athlete* will help lawyers go next level in their efforts to regain control over their careers. Dr. Wood shows us that with training, persistence, and practice, lawyers can attain psychological and physical health, better professional prospects, more joyful relationships, and greatly enhanced personal and professional satisfaction.

The approach Dr. Wood shares with us in *Lawyer Like an Athlete* is literally a career saver—and in some instances, a lifesaver. Every attorney, at any stage, should read this book.

—Joan M. Fortin, Esq.
Chief Executive Officer, Bernstein Shur

INTRODUCTION

I didn't go into psychology with the expectation that I'd specialize in attorney wellness. I started out with a Bachelor of Arts degree in communications that led me, after stints with two really exciting but financially strapped start-up magazines in Chicago, to being the Midwest advertising manager for a Dow Jones publication. What I thought would be a dream job with a firmly established, hugely reputable corporation turned into a wake-up call, as I noticed that many of my coworkers were unwell and unhappy from undue stress.

I'd observed one colleague literally doing three-martini lunches on a regular basis and steadily gaining weight, another going through a nasty divorce from chronically favoring her profession over family, and yet another suffering from mounting medical issues entirely related to insufficient self-care. These three colleagues were not much older than me, and I could see that their rock star status (those three-martini lunches often resulted in big sales) would soon slip from sacrificing too much for their careers. I'd become starkly aware of the toll ambition could take and wanted fiercely to rise above that calamity—without giving up my passion for demanding work.

With the goal of helping myself and my fellow high-achievers to not become casualties of high-intensity occupations, I decided to go back to school and earn my doctorate in psychology. I am endlessly curious about what it takes for especially enterprising people—not just attorneys but physicians, executives, politicians, et al.—to thrive in all respects as they strive to be the best. Becoming a psychologist was my way of learning how to be professionally stimulated *and* mentally, emotionally, and physically fit.

My attention started shifting from the private practice—where I worked with *all* driven, intellectually oriented professionals—to lawyers specifically about 10 years ago when an attorney friend in Florida mentioned her state bar had recently prioritized attorney wellness and could use some relevant continuing legal education (CLE) programming. I love producing webinars, and I was soon regularly facilitating them for the Florida Bar and then several other state bars as the attorney wellness trend picked up. Those webinars increasingly put me in touch with exasperated and worn-out attorneys struggling to hold onto their well-being when standard stress-reduction advice from self-help books and therapists couldn't seem to make a dent. Intrigued, I did my own study and found that attorney stress is so far outside the norm of what other stressed professionals experience that I decided to define it as "attorney outlier stress."

Which is when I really got fascinated.

As I've worked more and more with attorneys through CLE programming, one-on-one coaching, and law firm consulting, I've found that one of the things I have in common with a lot of lawyers is a love of mysteries and puzzles. Solving problems is my forte, and the more elusive the answer, the better. Naturally I've enjoyed figuring out answers to the questions attorneys most often bring me, similar to what may have brought you to this book:

Is it possible to be professionally accomplished and personally rewarded in a field considered more stressful than any other field?

And, if it *is* possible for attorneys to arrive at and sustain a full-bodied version of success amid relentless duress, how do they do it?

The answers to those questions began to emerge as an epiphany while I was watching Serena Williams on TV exuding her customary extraordinary levels of stamina, focus, utter hardiness, and staggering resolve.

I began to wonder: *What is it that catapults sports figures toward success despite tremendous odds?*

How do athletes manage to participate regularly in turbo-charged bodily and mental exertion while also staying at the summit of physical health, alertness, concentration, and motivation?

Suddenly I made a connection.

Just like elite athletes, attorneys are in a league of their own regarding the expectations placed on them and the higher-level-than-usual methods needed to help them thrive in the face of elevated pressure. Star athletes have a lot to teach attorneys about the importance of physical and mental health in building and sustaining the heightened resilience necessary to stay competitive in a cutthroat field. Strategies borrowed from the world of professional athletes are a natural fit for a profession requiring a similarly exceptional brand of endurance.

That Serena Williams moment led to many months of research, as I immersed myself in the kind of regimens athletes use to keep themselves sturdy and solid while achieving high-stakes goals. Customizing the game plans of elite athletes to the similarly onerous world of attorneys, *Lawyer Like an Athlete* is a culmination of all I've learned about helping attorneys to reach enviable levels of fulfillment and achievement incorporating the secrets of sports champions. I've been delivering the program presented in this book for a while now through my popular *Lawyer Like an Athlete* CLE workshops, so you can rest assured that the many strategies you'll be learning about—thought conditioning, internal/external balancing, and envisioning the win, to name a few—are well-tested and effective.

You can consider this book your own personal companion to help you thrive amid the rigors of lawyering so that you can actually have the sane, viable, and satisfying existence you dreamed about in law school. Because *Lawyer Like an Athlete* is designed to be a sensible, structured training manual, you will feel supported and encouraged as you move through your reading experience. Incrementally, little by little, your life will begin to unclench, and you will do away with the stresses that drain and obstruct so you can prosper in everything you do.

This is a book you can do on your own terms, at your own pace. Unlike your job, there is nothing mandatory about what I'm offering up here. There is no expectation that you read this book by a particular date or in a particular way. Your evolution is most likely to happen when you choose a schedule that appeals to you. Racing or forcing your way through the chapters will only add to the stress that drove you to pick this book up. The more relaxed you are as you delve into the material, the more you will be able to integrate what resonates.

Along the lines of effective athletic training, you are likely to gain most from *Lawyer Like an Athlete* if you apply new learning through action. Each chapter includes exercises so you can experiment, finesse, and see what results you get. For example, I might recommend that you tweak the way you're thinking about something, change up your morning routine a bit, or try a different tactic with a difficult person. Just like sequential weight training you might do at the gym, you will start with basic exercises and eventually ramp up to heavier lifting.

It may be helpful to keep in mind as you proceed that my occupation is helping people feel engaged and motivated as they tackle all manner of hardship. You can count on the pages ahead to keep you positive and hopeful, and you can trust that I get what lawyers go through because I've had a measure of success at helping attorneys with exactly what this book aims to do for you. We gain momentum from hearing the stories of others, so I make my suggestions relatable with portraits of clients who have overcome attorney-specific struggles like yours. Just like the attorneys I've already helped, you may be feeling a little wary as you begin—and yet slowly but surely you will gain the tools to make your life easier.

One final thing:

Have a little fun with this book. Let *Lawyer Like an Athlete* be a retreat from the obligations and expectations of work. Get in touch with your inner kid as you're reading, allowing a spirit of wonder and inquiry to pull you along. Take in only what transcends or enlivens, and let the rest stay on the page. Put the book down periodically, seek fresh water, fresh air, or fresh scenery, and come back revived. Interact with the book as a deserved, meaningful diversion—rather than one more thing weighing you down—and, regardless of where this reading adventure takes you, you are guaranteed to end up feeling lighter.

STAGE ONE

Preseason

1

Make the Cut

Most likely just reading the title of this first chapter is getting your adrenaline going. You're thinking of charismatic athletes flexing their muscles bigger than everyone else, leaving less powerful rivals cowering in the dust. As an attorney, you're recalling all you've done to make the cut in the legal world: surviving the ruthless Socratic law school teaching method, matching wits with hostile opposition in the courtroom, saying yes to clients no matter what they ask, plowing through work no matter what the cost. For many diehard attorneys, making the cut means boasting that you work effectively under unrelenting duress and with such 24/7 persistence that you don't have a life.

In this case though, making the cut means something much more admirable than wearing workaholism like a badge of courage. It means acknowledging first that athletes who make the cut are able to outshine fellow contenders because they have prepared themselves to be at the top of their game. Making the cut in professional sports means being in superb enough physical and mental form to stand out in the ring. Athletes who train too hard and disregard proper nutrition, ample rest, mental vigor, and other integral components of physical greatness may burn brightly at first from sheer talent. But even the most promising prowess gives way when it is not consistently fortified for excellence.

> "Making the cut means something much more admirable than wearing workaholism like a badge of courage."

Any athlete aspiring to be a champion must understand that if they are to succeed, they must make their career their utmost priority and organize their life around it to maximize their competitive edge. Specifically, an athlete intent on making the cut must put the extraordinarily exacting work of training and competing at the center of their lives in the service of sustained success.

These four keys to athletic championship are equally integral to attorney awesomeness. My Attorney in Action vignettes give you real-life examples to draw on:

Exquisite Self-Care: Serious athletes get plenty of rest and sleep, eat in ways that bolster the body and brain, set appropriate boundaries with people and technology, take breaks and vacations, and enjoy excess in manageable, celebratory doses.

Grounded Perspective: Serious athletes keep their minds focused and sharp by untethering themselves from disruptive internal chatter in response to everything from criticism about their own performance to unsettling news about a world event. By changing their own self-talk, they also reduce the impact of potentially rattling situations. They take in the full picture—good and bad—and choose to see solutions.

Nourishing Diversions: Serious athletes turn their attention away from work regularly to exercise their imagination, walk in nature, play with their kids, meander around the house, and generally give their hardworking brains a holiday by thinking—or not thinking—in different and enjoyable ways.

Thriving Relationships: Serious athletes get that human beings are social animals that reach their potential when they are supported and encouraged by each other. They make ample time and space for building and furthering relationships at home and work because they know the motivating, reassuring, connecting force of fellowship. They engage others in cooperation and collaboration, always communicating appreciation, addressing conflict respectfully, regularly hanging out with their favorite people, and minimizing interactions with people who even remotely deplete them.

Attorney in Action

Inundated entertainment attorney Ethan revealed at his second coaching session with me that a colleague had told him he should stop wasting money on coaching and just drink more alcohol to reduce stress instead. He emphasized that remarks like this—all coming from a toxic belief that self-care is fruitless for attorneys—made it hard for him to believe that my *Lawyer Like an Athlete* program could really work. I suggested it takes time to change beliefs, especially in the face of scoffing critics, and he decided to keep coming. He gained confidence in coaching as he tried small experiments, like getting rid of distracting alerts on his phone and closing down work 10 minutes earlier than usual. Though his professional responsibilities were still there, they began to seem less daunting.

Here's what that work-plus model looks like for a sports champion:

Attorney in Action

Associate Eliot, perpetually walking on eggshells because of an overly faultfinding senior partner, had already been to two psychologists who hadn't helped when he came to his first coaching appointment with me. He admitted he had been ready to give up on my profession, convinced we (psychologists) do more harm than good to attorneys, when a persuasive colleague had referred him to me. As we worked together, Eliot began to realize that he couldn't change that partner's unreasonable standards, but he could learn to deal with him constructively. He became his own best cheerleader and soon felt less demoralized by speaking rationally to himself in the face of scrutiny: *I do good work despite inevitable mistakes. Screwups are an opportunity to learn and grow.*

Attorney in Action

Delaney, a tax attorney, emailed me after a webinar I'd presented highlighting the importance of interests outside of work to say, "You obviously don't understand attorneys. It's not realistic for us to do these things." Two months later, she emailed me again with an update: despite her skepticism, she'd tried getting up from her desk a few times every day to go outside and look up at the sky. By escaping from the intensity of her work in these small doses, her schedule and inner world somehow seemed more spacious, and she adopted other kinds of breaks—walking a neighbor's dog sometimes, listening to classical music while driving—to untighten her mind.

Just like admired athletes, the most successful attorneys accelerate their career performance with stamina, enthusiasm, and self-assuredness infused by a satisfying and enriching surrounding life. That old-school lawyering philosophy that making the cut means working more than your competition, taking the edge off in extreme ways, fighting aggression with aggression, and sacrificing personal fulfillment for the cause is getting exposed as a ticket to unhappiness and exhaustion as the attorney stress problem escalates. The lesson for attorneys is this: athletes outperform others not by working excessively but by priming themselves to work smarter. In the same way, priming yourself for excellence is entirely dependent on your commitment to the essential components surrounding your work:

Attorney in Action

Kim, a divorce attorney, told me at a workshop that she was all too familiar with marriages falling apart from neglect. Her husband had been complaining that he was tired of being second to her job, and she didn't know how she could turn that around given the unavoidable long workdays that left her feeling completely spent. I suggested that she could change things for the better by making it her evening priority to enjoy quality time with her husband. She found that she felt closer to her husband from their more intentional interactions, and the much-needed time-outs helped Kim to relax, recharge, and really be bolstered by her husband's support.

> "Just like admired athletes, the most successful attorneys accelerate their career performance with stamina, enthusiasm, and self-assuredness infused by a satisfying and enriching surrounding life."

The most effective performance enhancers aren't caffeine and protein shakes, but getting out of your office, reveling in recreation, letting your mind roam, and being with people who have nothing to do with law.

How does it feel to consider that true performance enhancers are your physical condition, mindset, downtime, and relationships—*if* you tend to them with the devotion you give work?

And what are the components around lawyering that will bring out *your* best?

If you're like most of the attorneys I coach, it is very likely that you have never encountered a situation where work is still at the center, but all around you are factors that give you a fuller life and power your output. In fact, you may be scratching your head right now because you've been bombarded for so long by the prevailing self-help wisdom that you should be less obsessive about work.

My guess is you have probably heard experts suggest that you stop thinking about lawyering entirely if you want to be happier and healthier. You may have resisted getting a hobby and spending more time with family because you've learned to look at self-care, human connection, mental distance, and other pursuits not overtly linked to billable hours as shirking responsibility. You've probably seen people you know benefit from taking work less seriously, but you realize less seriousness is not possible given the high-stakes, all-out rigorous nature of lawyering.

> "You may never have encountered a situation where work is still at the center, but all around you are factors that give you a fuller life and power your output."

As you consider adopting a success model used effectively by elite professional athletes who are under the gun to such an extent that work must never be neglected, you may be feeling buoyed. You might also be feeling some relief because, finally, you're getting agreement from an attorney wellness expert that taking

> “As you consider adopting a success model used effectively by elite professional athletes who are under the gun to such an extent that work must never be neglected, you may be feeling buoyed.”

the emphasis off make-or-break work is more likely to amplify stress rather than reduce it.

But, as much as you may be opening to the idea of turning standard stress-reduction advice on its head to be at your best, you are also likely thinking that this model sounds nice but it's not practical because there's still the matter of drowning in professional obligations. You may be thinking it's not feasible to do these things I'm suggesting because, though you get the logic of priming yourself for excellence, you will lose clients if you are less available to them, or you will lose clout with colleagues if you take time away from work to take care of yourself and have a little fun. You may also be thinking that the old-school version of making the cut is too entrenched in your profession for you to change it and that you must toe the line. You may even be thinking that you'll get fired for going against the status quo.

Whatever you are thinking, the important thing to keep in mind at this juncture is that you don't need to make any decisions just yet. For now, if making the cut in a more sustainable way sounds intriguing, jotting down responses to these prompts may help you begin to pave the way:

LIST ONE OR TWO THINGS YOU CAN DO TO IMPROVE ON:

Taking care of yourself: (Million-dollar skier Mikaela Shiffrin always opts for seltzer and cranberry juice when offered alcohol at social events.[1]) What self-care practice might work for you?

____

____

____

[1] Hilary Brueck, “Million-Dollar Skier Mikaela Shiffrin ‘Almost Never’ Drinks Coffee, Rarely Has Alcohol, and Gets at Least 9 Hours of Sleep. Here's the Science Behind Her Winning Strategy,” *Business Insider*, June 12, 2019, https://www.businessinsider.com/diet-sleep-habits-olympic-skier-mikaela-shiffrin-2019-6.

Thinking in ways that encourage you: (As part of what he calls his Mental Power Game, Tiger Woods reminds himself in tough moments that every future moment is an opportunity to improve his situation.[2]) What could you say to rally yourself when you're tense and pressed?

____

____

____

Turning your attention from work to activities that revive you mentally: (Some A-list football players routinely give their playbooking brains respite by playing chess, and they're better on the field because of it.[3]) What can you do to give your attorney brain some time off so that you can come back sharper?

____

____

____

Having good relationships: (Olympic swimmer Michael Phelps bonds with his kids through a yoga exercise that helps them all unwind.[4]) How might you enjoy being with the people you love?

____

____

____

As we conclude this first chapter, you have probably become aware that my *Lawyer Like an Athlete* program allows room for your individual

---

[2] David MacKenzie, "The Power of Tiger Woods' Mental Game," Instruction for the Mental Game of Golf, March 15, 2021, https://golfstateofmind.com/tiger-woods-mental-game-power/.

[3] Robert O'Donnell, "Forget Madden. The Hottest Game in the N.F.L. Is Chess," *The New York Times*, October 10, 2022, https://www.nytimes.com/2022/10/11/sports/football/nfl-chess-blitzchamps.html.

[4] Steven Vargas, "Michael Phelps Credits Wife Nicole Johnson with Helping Him Through Anxiety and Depression Struggles," *E! Online*, May 5, 2022, https://www.eonline.com/news/1329860/michael-phelps-credits-wife-nicole-johnson-with-helping-him-through-anxiety-and-depression-struggles.

likes and dislikes. As long as you adhere to the fundamental work-plus model, possibilities for energizing your career through exquisite self-care, a more grounded perspective, nourishing diversions, and thriving relationships are endless. Customizing the model to suit your unique desires and disposition may be overwhelming at first as you gain new knowledge and ideas begin to spark, but trust me, you will eventually distill the model down to a tailored paradigm that is true to you.

Now, I recommend you take however long a break you need to let all this new information settle and see what dissipates, what bubbles up. In the next chapter, we'll cover the essentials of bringing pie-in-the-sky dreams down to earth with effective goal-setting.

2

Break It Down

Most attorneys come to coaching with perfectly reasonable aspirations. However, when they present their goals—"I want to reduce my stress"; "I want more time to do what I want to be doing"; "I need more balance"—it always comes down to a desire to consistently experience work and life differently. Reason goes right out the window, though, when attorneys tell me how quickly they expect to accomplish these perfectly reasonable results, as if personal and professional improvement can happen on demand.

Whether they want to stick to an eating plan, deal better with hostility, or have a more manageable schedule, what's always hard for an attorney to hear from me at the end of a first session is that the improved circumstances they seek won't happen overnight. As Michael Jordan, whose own memoir emphasizes the pitfalls of too-big jumps, puts it, "Step by step. I can't see any other way of accomplishing anything."[1]

To have lofty goals and want to realize them quickly is a natural and positive part of being an exceptionally driven professional, especially in an increasingly impatient, quick-fix-oriented culture. After all, we are accustomed in our modern world to inventions, ranging from microwaves to increasingly smarter phones to driverless cars, that let us do the things we want faster and faster. No matter how quickly we can make dinner, transmit information, or get a package delivered, human beings are still human

[1] Siamak Vahidi, "Michael Jordan," *The National Research Center on the Gifted and Talented* (1990-2013), June 17, 2015, https://nrcgt.uconn.edu/underachievement_study/self-efficacy/se_jordan/#.

Attorney in Action

It's fair to say that Nelson was close to hyperventilating when he sat down on my couch for the first time. He described feeling on top of the world two years ago when he'd been offered a job at a huge New York law firm, but recently while working alone at home on yet another Saturday, he'd looked down from his high-rise apartment window at people walking around doing regular Saturday things and realized he didn't want this crazy, workaholic lifestyle any longer. Since then, he'd been vacillating between fiercely believing he could find a job that would allow him a life and feeling evermore mired in misery because he didn't know how to make the transition happen instantly. Once I helped him to get off the madly swinging pendulum and get centered through verbal processing and relaxation techniques, Nelson saw the wisdom of replacing his go-from-A-to-Z-this-minute approach with a more sensible game plan. Then he was able to start moving forward in small increments—talk to a friend who had recently made a satisfying job change, dig out his resume, make a list of possible new jobs he might want to check out—to progressively unmoor himself.

beings, and so more complex inner-oriented endeavors, like surrounding your work with nutritive components, only happen from the block-by-block building of new and more empowering skills and habits.

Breaking down goals into manageable phases isn't exactly a sexy-sounding prospect for anyone who loves the thrill of achievement. Believe me, I get it. But if you want to see lasting change as you retool your life to empower your career, a conservative approach will be far more effective than making dramatic strides.

> "If you want to see lasting change as you retool your life to empower your career, a conservative approach will be far more effective than making dramatic strides."

Think about it for a minute.

All the proficiencies you acquired as a child before you started demanding on-the-spot results from yourself came gradually. Very gradually. You learned everything from walking and talking to riding your bike and doing chores through a series of very small shifts and stages.

You moved from writing your name to writing term papers, from adding 2 + 2 to figuring geometric theorems throughout several grades, countless instructions, and a multitude of homework assignments. You gained greater knowledge and mastery because you had lessons that were structured: challenging enough to be stimulating but not so challenging that you froze in fear at the very thought of advancing through them.

Like children who haven't yet bought into the cockeyed adult logic that says small steps aren't worth the effort because they won't really get you anywhere, career athletes really have an edge over attorneys here. As 18-time Iron Man finisher and elite endurance coach Patrick McCrann tells his champing-at-the-bit clients, "Dream big and execute small. Just as race day is thousands of footsteps from the start to the finish, your training should be, too."[2]

It's true for all athletes: if not for their adherence to tediously planned-out training programs and tireless repetition designed to move them sequentially from one level to the next over many years, they would never, ever achieve champion status. A Little Leaguer going straight to the World Series is as ridiculous to fathom as climbing from the first rung of a tall ladder to the top rung with no rungs in between—or moving from law school graduation to full partner in one full, seamless sweep.

By now you are probably thinking, "I get the whole athlete thing. But if I take small steps, it'll take way too long to reach my goals."

Well, I understand where you're coming from, but I want to assure you that taking small steps actually helps you achieve your goals more readily than you ever thought possible.

Here's why:

Whereas big steps can sap your strength and stamina by triggering draining emotions like anxiety and self-doubt, small steps encourage the emotions and energy that invigorate real growth and accomplishment. Rebelling against an established lawyer culture of workaholism to put yourself first may send you into a panic, but a first step of placing an inspirational quote on your bulletin board may nudge you toward feeling more worthy of better treatment. Likewise, whereas the possibility of reversing entrenched, unproductive ways of coping with stress may send you into a

---

[2] Patrick McCrann, "8 Baby Steps to the Marathon for Beginners," ACTIVE.com, September 9, 2013, https://www.active.com/running/articles/8-baby-steps-to-the-marathon-for-beginners.

> "The beauty of a small step is simply that it lets you get out of indecision, second-guessing, and procrastination and *get started.*"

shame spiral, the first step of looking online for a new gym you might like may stir some enthusiasm.

The beauty of a small step is simply that it lets you get out of indecision, second-guessing, and procrastination and *get started.* Once that first small stride is taken, you feel more confident, motivated, and ready for step number two, step number three, and so on, and your goal begins to manifest. All you have to do to get going is decide on a series of steps so ridiculously, laughably, insanely doable that hesitancy doesn't stand a chance of getting in your way.

Now, some things to keep in mind as you consider how you might accomplish your goals more effectively using the tiny-step method:

First, no matter how minuscule the steps are, you won't be successful with a goal unless you're really excited about it. Professional athletes

Attorney in Action

Christine, a new lawyer fresh out of law school, told me at our first session that she felt overwhelmed for the first time in her life. She recounted making law review and being at the top of her graduating law school class simply by meeting expectations. "And now," she said with exasperation, "I look at the incredible distance between where I am and my definition of success, and I have no idea what to do first." After discussing one of the biggest adjustments of moving from law school to the real world, namely no syllabi or study aids or standard resume-building options laid out for her, Christine realized she was now looking at a whole career of growth without those year-by-year academic guidelines she had come to rely on. By participating in twice-per-month coaching sessions, she began to whittle down her long-term agenda into doable steps. She decided to start by taking one key colleague to lunch per week over the next several weeks, a process that allowed her to bond with her peers while drawing support from senior colleagues who had already made the adjustment she was immersed in. Stimulating conversations over lunch gave her plenty of ideas for further small steps she could take to direct her work and life.

who aren't 100 percent passionate about what they're doing don't stand a chance of being successful because, just like lawyering, professional sports take everything you've got. What this translates to is that no matter how much you want to accomplish something for someone else, you won't be able to keep it going if you're not completely on board. So, if you really want to be healthier because you want to please your physician and your family, but you're not ready to give up smoking, your goal of healthier lungs won't work. If you want a higher salary but you really don't want the responsibilities of moving up at your firm, then your goal of making partner probably won't get you the long-term results you're after. Being an attorney is hard enough; don't make it harder by working on nonmandatory goals you're not interested in.

Another important thing to consider about goals is that they can be accomplished more efficiently when you reward yourself along the way. When you don't do this, either because you consider rewards kid stuff or not worth the money or because you don't think you deserve or need compensation for your work, you risk losing momentum at best and sabotaging your success at worst. The cool thing here is that compensation doesn't have to be complicated to provide a powerful incentive. Rewards can be anything meaningful to you—a new music download, a favorite magazine, a bike ride through your favorite neighborhood, a nap—that you give yourself as a gift for a job well done. (Just make sure your rewards are aligned with your outcome; rewarding yourself with a pizza when you're trying to go down a size is a misalignment.)

To stay motivated and charged as you move forward, particularly when you're working on something unpleasant but unavoidable, encourage yourself with appealing incentives bit by bit, much like you'd reward a dog with biscuits as it learns a new trick. Then, when you've reached your final goal, you can reward yourself more handsomely: perhaps buying a special piece of art when you've organized your office, arranging a spa day for yourself after you've cleaned out the garage, or subscribing to a season at the local theater when you've overcome your TV addiction.

One more thing to consider about goal-setting is that you will occasionally slip up, and that's okay and to be expected because, after all, you are human. The solution is to review your tiny-step plan at these times and ask yourself if the steps need revising. Maybe your next step is too big and you need to scale it down. Maybe your rewards aren't incentivizing enough. Or maybe your overall goal isn't doing it for you anymore and you want to focus on something else.

Attorney in Action

Max, an experienced real estate attorney, was referred to coaching by his firm because, though he was loved by his colleagues and clients, he was way behind on getting contracts out the door. He told me his favorite part of work was meeting new clients and helping them realize their dreams, but he detested any kind of paperwork, and just thinking about the ever-growing "past due" pile on his credenza—work that he couldn't delegate—was making him nauseous. Together we came up with a way to get through the backlog that seemed reasonable: Max agreed to set a timer for five minutes and deal with the paperwork until the alarm went off, then reward himself by watching a favorite comedian on YouTube for five minutes. He did this three times before our next session and not only got through the five minutes of dreaded paperwork each time but actually went on for a half-hour one of those times because he figured, what the heck, he was already doing it and it wasn't so bad. By continuing with the tiny-step approach, the backlog became less intimidating, and Max became habitually more proactive with contracts.

A final consideration about this tiny-step approach: adults learn by doing, not reading, listening, or watching. The idea here is that every time you are putting a step into motion, you are integrating new information. With each digestible tiny step, you are progressively showing your neuropathways how to drift in the direction of your desired endpoint. Even if it's just an inch forward, it is movement, and with movement comes progress.

Now that you're considerably more up on the art of attainment, let's revisit the work-plus model we discussed in the last chapter.

LIST THREE TINY STEPS YOU CAN TAKE TO:

Boost your self-care: (You might say no to sweets twice this week or Google massage therapists in your area.)

1. ____________________
2. ____________________
3. ____________________

Think in ways that encourage you: (You could make a list of your top five qualities or recall one thing that has already gone well today.)

1. ______________________________
2. ______________________________
3. ______________________________

Turn your attention from work to activities that revive you mentally: (You could get up and stretch sometime today or do a quick crossword puzzle.)

1. ______________________________
2. ______________________________
3. ______________________________

Have good relationships: (You might text a friend what you appreciate about them or say hello to a colleague you don't normally greet.)

1. ______________________________
2. ______________________________
3. ______________________________

Keeping in mind that rewards will ease your way forward, vow to treat yourself for the small strides you've made so far in your *Lawyer Like an Athlete* journey. Whether you've acted on any of the tiny steps you've come up with or have only written them down, you deserve recognition for getting this far.

As we close this chapter, the big takeaway is that the most spectacular wins are most likely to emerge from a series of small wins. Having gotten out of your head that you must realize your goals and dreams right now, this minute, you are likely less stressed than you were when you started this chapter. Armed with the tiny-step method, you are in a better position to begin the next chapter, which addresses another essential part of lawyering like an athlete: putting your focus on what's most integral to your success and keeping it there.

3

Keep Your Head in the Game

There are plenty of jobs people can do without having to worry too much about being distracted. If your work is placing modest demands on you, your full attention may not always be required, and so you can put it elsewhere. On the other hand, consider that Jakobi Meyers, New England Patriots wide receiver, made the "biggest blunder in football history" by absent-mindedly tossing the football to an opposing player.[1] One split second of inattention in a high-pressure job is all it takes to blow a game.

For athletes who must be totally tuned in, acutely aware of what is happening around them, "the ability to marshal one's own attention is arguably the new superpower," says sports scientist Paul Gamble, Ph.D.[2]

Likewise for attorneys.

In a career that asks way more from the human brain than most, you must master the art of keeping your full attention on what's important.

And in a world where we are unceasingly disrupted by a continuous bombardment of information and noise, that takes real mental muscle.

Can you even imagine LeBron James, Shohei Ohtani, or Megan Rapinoe being so lackadaisical about where their attention goes that they are routinely pulled away from their training, rigorous practice, and nourishment of their gift, and instead sucked into scrolling, texting, gaming, and bingeing?

---

[1] Mike Thomas, "Jakobi Meyers Made 1 of the Biggest Blunders in NFL History, but He Didn't Run From It," Sportscasting | Pure Sports, December 9, 2022, https://www.sportscasting.com/jakobi-meyers-made-1-of-the-biggest-blunders-in-nfl-history-but-he-didnt-run-from-it/.

[2] Paul Gamble, "Dealing with Distraction," Prepared Athlete Training & Health, March 5, 2021, https://preparedathlete.info/prepared-blog/dealing-with-distraction.

Can you picture these incredible athletes craving the dopamine rush of an incoming text, wondering if there might be something more interesting happening someplace else if only they could check their phones *right now*?

Because digital dependence is the biggest attention-eroder out there, athletes work hard to not get sucked in. And your biggest opportunity for building your focus is to get a firm grip on your own technology use.

The first step is acknowledging (as all athletes do) that your gadgets are designed to be addictive, and thus you are probably using them in ways that are compromising your concentration. Then you must examine your relationship with technology, eliminate what is not helpful, and, in a highly discerning manner, decide what you can take from it to make your life and work more satisfying and productive. For example, stop shopping online for the thrill, and optimize that convenience by buying online only what you genuinely need and can't find elsewhere; do play online games if that's a recharging reward for you, but don't play games as a way to procrastinate. By exercising limits with technology, using what serves you, and letting the rest fall away, you will find yourself feeling less intruded upon, freer to move, and in a better position to eliminate other, more internal distractions.

Here's how that goes:

When an attorney tells me they don't have time for anything but work, I ask them for a rundown of their technology use.

I pose two questions to them:

- *How much of your technology use helps you to be happier and more productive?*
- *How much of your technology use is detrimental?*

> "By exercising limits with technology, using what serves you, and letting the rest fall away, you will find yourself feeling less intruded upon, freer to move, and in a better position to eliminate other, more internal distractions."

At first, they insist their relationship with technology is all good: scrolling through Instagram helps them feel connected, responding to the phone whenever it rings is part of being an attorney, and watching Netflix is a great way to unwind. When I push attorneys further, though, they are dismayed to realize that looking at social media is creating a sense of isolation over connection, being literally "on call" throughout the day is curtailing the deep thought necessary for providing worthwhile legal assistance, and TV is more numbing than it is relaxing. When they think about it, activities involving technology, if not chosen and managed with an eye for the perfect synthesis of gratification and industriousness, steal not only attention but a whole lot of fulfillment.

I frame it this way:

Wouldn't it be wonderful if, by reducing your technology use to only what truly pleases and propels you, you could free up your calendar for all those things you say you don't have room for?

You've been pondering where you would get the time to put into those four critical work-plus model components of a sustainable law career, and now you have it. Be matter-of-fact with yourself about how much technological involvement is not only unnecessary but is getting in the way of attaining what you really want. Because technology is so insidious, seducing you away from what's really important without you even realizing it sometimes, robbing you from right under your nose, you need to take complete charge of your attention span and wrest back control. The bottom line is that you can't research meticulously, craft bulletproof legal arguments, think on your feet in the courtroom, or meet other tough calls of lawyering if you're just partially paying attention.

Once you take full responsibility for what you focus on, ignoring everything not truly relevant to you and your goals, you will work more efficiently with higher mental acuity, and the really appealing by-product will be a looser schedule. University College Dublin cognitive psychology professor Aidan Moran compared this kind of attentional command, which professional athletes possess, to a spotlight that you can put where you want and never lose.[3]

"Once you take full responsibility for what you focus on, ignoring everything not truly relevant to you and your goals, you will work more efficiently with higher mental acuity, and the really appealing by-product will be a looser schedule."

[3] Aidan Moran, "Practical Techniques for Improving Concentration Skills in Athletes," nzequestrian.org, July 25, 2009, https://www.nzequestrian.org.nz/wp-content/uploads/Practical-Techniques-for-Improving-Concentration-Skills-in-Athletes.pdf.

Attorney in Action

When recounting her typical technology use, tax attorney Toni told me at our first session that she liked looking at Facebook every day to stay current. She described this ritual as necessary to keep in touch and break away a bit from work. When I asked her to think about any drawbacks of this habit, it occurred to her that looking at Facebook actually had the effect of making her feel envious of friends who, based on their posted photos, were getting more time off than she was. I suggested that she look at Facebook a little less during the next two weeks. The result? Toni found that she freed up time for reading fiction, a considerably more enjoyable activity she didn't think she could fit in.

Pretty nice to imagine, huh?

We'll go over other sidetracking culprits later in this chapter—technology is not the only way you're throwing away time—but for now, let's look at some immediate ways you can give yourself breathing room.

Completing the Technology Inventory below will illuminate your relationship with the digital devices in your life. You'll begin to see how you might make adjustments to galvanize your focus and create the time you need to lawyer like an athlete.

TECHNOLOGY INVENTORY

List all the ways you use your phone at work:

____

____

____

Of all the ways you use your phone at work, which ones most contribute to you being at your best professionally?

____

____

____

Of all the ways you use your phone at work, which are the least critical and actually get in the way of you being at your professional best?

____

____

____

List all the ways you use your laptop at work:

____

____

____

Of all the ways you use your laptop at work, which ones most contribute to you being at your best professionally?

____

____

____

Of all the ways you use your laptop at work, which are the least critical and actually get in the way of you being at your professional best?

____

____

____

List any ways you could start using your phone and laptop to make you less stressed and more successful at work:

____

____

____

List all the ways you use your phone in your personal life:

____

____

____

Of all the ways you use your phone in your personal life, which ones contribute to you being at your personal best?

____

____

____

Of all the ways you use your phone in your personal life, which are the least critical and actually get in the way of you being at your personal best?

____

____

____

List all the ways you use your laptop in your personal life:

____

____

____

Of all the ways you use your laptop in your personal life, which ones contribute to you being at your personal best?

____

____

____

Of all the ways you use your laptop in your personal life, which are the least critical and actually get in the way of you being at your personal best?

____

____

____

List all the ways you use your TV in your personal life:

____

____

____

Of all the ways you use your TV in your personal life, which ones contribute to you being at your personal best?

____

____

Of all the ways you use your TV in your personal life, which are the least critical and actually get in the way of you being at your personal best?

____

____

List any ways you're not using your phone, laptop, and TV that could make your life easier and more satisfying:

____

____

Once you've completed the inventory, go through it again with greater tenacity, just to make sure you've got it all down. In the words of athletic coach Erica Suter, the gist of what you should be asking yourself is this: "Who are you going to unfollow to clear out your head?" and "Who are you going to follow to infuse value into your life?"[4] No excuses, no buts, no rationalizing.

Next, remembering that handy tiny-step method from Chapter 2, come up with a specific plan you can implement to start reducing your technology use to what's vital. Consider how you can begin to call the technology shots and raise the bar for what deserves and warrants your precious attention.

IDENTIFY THREE TINY STEPS TO . . .

Use technology more judiciously at work: (For example, designate specific times each day to check email/texts/voicemail instead of randomly checking throughout the day; eliminate news text alerts; try to cut back on social media scrolling.)

1. ______________________________
2. ______________________________
3. ______________________________

---

[4] Erica Suter, "Helping Youth Athletes with Social Media Distraction," Erica Suter, January 19, 2020, https://ericasuter.com/helping-youth-athletes-with-social-media-distractions/.

Use technology more judiciously at home: (Buy a watch so you don't have to look at your phone for the time; check social media only once per day for no more than a half-hour; reduce gaming/TV.)

1. ______________________________
2. ______________________________
3. ______________________________

Now remember, there's no need to act on anything just yet. At this stage, you're simply collecting ideas and contemplating new possibilities. Before you commit to taking any tiny steps you've come up with, let's build on your awareness of how you're unintentionally misusing, maybe even abusing, your focus.

These suggestions will help you to channel your awareness more deliberately so that you can have a healthier attention span. This means you'll get more work done in less time, thereby increasing your availability to apply all four components of the work-plus model: taking care of yourself, improving your mindset, tending to your relationships, and participating in fortifying pastimes.

First, face reality. Sigmund Freud was a bit eccentric, but one thing he got undeniably right is that human beings go to impressive lengths to avoid truths they do not want to accept. While it is

Attorney in Action

Law firm partner Dean complained at our first session that he was working 70 or more hours every week, never getting home early enough to have dinner with his family. He explained that he'd tried every way possible to reduce his work hours but hadn't been successful because he was always getting pulled off course by urgent texts and calls coming through his phone. He'd been making an effort to check his phone only at certain times but found that just looking at his phone could draw him in. When he took my advice to put his phone in a drawer during times reserved for high-level work, he realized that the visual cue alone of his phone had been a big distraction. He now finds that just by putting gadgets away when he is not using them, he can considerably reduce back-and-forth checking and is able to get home for dinner with his family a couple of nights per week.

easier in the short run to pretend your troubled marriage is fine or to ignore scary symptoms rather than go to the doctor, there is a long-term cost to keeping painful realities at bay. The longer you dodge inconvenient truths, the more wherewithal you must put into repressing and denying what is happening, and the fewer inner resources you have for making the most of the moment you're in. You can be considerably less stressed by acknowledging any realities, such as relationship, health, and financial problems that you're pushing out of your awareness, and then bringing them to the surface where you can responsibly address them.

What's a reality you can face to free up your time and attention?

____

____

____

Practice sensible multitasking. Have you ever tried to look interested in a Zoom meeting while checking your email? Have you ever attempted to eavesdrop on a nearby conversation while speaking to a dinner companion? Most of us learn from ample life experience that it's not feasible to give our full attention to two demanding activities at the same time. We know quite well that we pick up only fractured pieces and don't integrate the whole of anything when we dilute our regard like that, but we prefer to buy into the myth that we can do everything at once. The smartest

Attorney in Action

Dru, who came to me for coaching after taking a new job as an attorney at a nonprofit, was more stressed than usual about the process of getting acclimated. She found that her stress was exacerbated by second thoughts she was having over accepting a position with a lower salary, which meant she couldn't contribute as much as she always had to her household. By revisiting the topic with her wife, she gained reassurance that she had made the right choice. Her wife emphasized that she cared more about Dru's happiness than the amount of her paycheck. Once she was able to release her misgivings, Dru could focus more fully on settling into her new job.

attorneys know that stretching attention too thin to finish things faster ultimately wastes time due to all the mistakes and missed details you have to follow up on later. Multitasking absolutely can be effective but only when you do it sensibly by blending two low-focus activities, such as returning social texts while standing in line at the grocery store or listening to an audiobook while cleaning your workspace.

Name two low-focus activities that you could do together without stretching your attention span too far:

1. ______________________________
2. ______________________________

Deal with your baggage. Another attention sapper that you may not be cognizant of is unresolved business from your past. It could be childhood trauma you haven't sufficiently worked through, an apology you haven't made, a grievance you haven't dropped, or something crucial you haven't explored. Whatever it is, I promise you that it is weakening your focus on what's in front of you now. Once you start to deal with it—whether that means calling a friend, booking an appointment with a therapist, or writing a letter—doing so will let you put down whatever is haunting you so that you can operate from a more present place more often.

Write a step you can take toward resolving an issue from your past:

____

____

____

Get rid of clutter. A major source of distraction in our high-consumption culture is stuff: actual tangible items and the flow of information that never stops coming and keeps piling up. All that stuff takes up a lot of room and can be quite distracting. So, if you want a clear head, make sure to clear out the items that are occupying too much space in your life. You likely have clothes in your closet you don't wear, contraptions in your kitchen you don't need, books and professional journals you are never going to read, and objects you are keeping out of sheer obligation. By removing the obstacles that are blocking your success, you will feel less constricted and maneuver beyond what is cramping your style.

List three things you can toss to clear your space:

1. ______________________________
2. ______________________________
3. ______________________________

Take care of petty annoyances. It's the small things nagging at us, all those pesky errands, little loose ends, minor chores, that add up and get in the way of our day. While there are some solutions we can't rush in life, we can pretty quickly reduce distraction by ticking off those seemingly weightless "to-do" list items. Simple acts like returning a library book, sending a thank-you note, or unsubscribing from an email list you don't want to be on can easily join together to create a palpable sense of relief.

Two petty annoyances you can check off your list:

1. ______________________________
2. ______________________________

Drop commitments no longer serving you. Another potential area of meaningless interruption is anything you've agreed to do that you are no longer enthusiastic about. Perhaps you joined a certain professional committee out of passion, and now you've lost interest. Or maybe you used to look forward to having lunch with a college friend once every month, but that's seeming like too much. In a continuously changing culture, with new ideas constantly making their way into your consciousness, you are bound to outgrow things. Any guilt you feel about that is just preventing you from going forward with whatever more appealing pursuit is calling you. The more you eliminate the commitments you've moved beyond, the more tuned in you will be with what matters most to you today.

One obligation you can excuse yourself from:

____

____

____

Now that you've looked at all the immediate opportunities you have for working more constructively and creating the time you need for yourself, let's go over strategies—all used by professional athletes—for optimizing your focus even more:

Ground yourself in your senses. Your capacity to converge resolutely on your work can be fortified by going deep in other ways when you're not working. This means getting out of your thinking brain and delving under surface distractions into activities that absorb you on a substantial level. Beach volleyball Olympian Lauren Fendrick likes to escape the ceaseless cacophony of everyday life by going into the sensations of cooking while listening to music.[5] Reaching that deeper, more pleasing place can happen by simply stopping what you're doing and asking yourself at random times: what am I feeling, seeing, smelling, hearing, or tasting right now? When you regularly expand your involvement with whatever is happening, noticing textures, colors, aromas, and sounds, you will be less inclined to skate from one disruption to the next.

Meditate. Kobe Bryant, who swore by disciplined meditation, said, "If I don't do it, it feels like I'm constantly chasing the day, as opposed to dictating the day."[6] Let me begin by assuring you that meditation is not a one-hour-a-day thing that involves sitting on a mat with your legs crossed, entirely emptying your mind, and feeling utterly at peace. In fact, no matter what you may have heard, evacuating your head, for a species noted for its capacity to analyze, is totally impossible and not the point anyway. The goal of meditation, which can be accomplished just about anywhere in as little as a few minutes a few times a week, is to get outside the racket of your busy life, close your eyes, and simply step back and observe your thinking. Whether your thoughts are racing or drifting or doing somersaults, it's by merely

---

[5] Sarah Sekula, "How Six Top Athletes Relax and Recover," *ESPN.com*, April 19, 2017, https://www.espn.com/espnw/life-style/story/_/id/19193888/how-six-top-athletes-relax-recover.

[6] Sean Grabowski, "Celebrities and Athletes Who Meditate Every Day," *The Mindful Steward*, September 14, 2023, https://themindfulsteward.com/celebrities-and-athletes-who-meditate-everyday/.

witnessing them that you begin to see that you have no control over your thoughts, but you are a decision-maker separate from your thoughts, and so you do get to decide how (or how not) to respond to them. As you increasingly see from meditation that your thoughts can do whatever they want to do and you don't need to answer to all of them, you begin to feel more in charge out in the world.

Let your mind roam. With all this emphasis on eliminating distractions for the sake of laser focus, it's wise to note that your brain needs time off between periods of prolonged concentration to rest. Breaking away from deep work has the huge benefit of getting your head out of routine thinking patterns so that new neural connections—thoughts veering from regular routes and combining in innovative and imaginative ways—get formed. While intense work is necessary to get things done, surprisingly amazing ideas come up when you're taking a shower, wandering through a museum, or walking in the woods. Professional skydiver Roberta Mancino steps off the tightrope of concentration by swimming in the ocean.[7] How can you let your own mind drift?

Before we end, an important caveat:

If you find as you aim to remove distractions from your life that there is still never enough time, your mind is always jumping around, and you have trouble focusing and finishing things, it *could be* that you have attention-deficit/hyperactivity disorder (ADHD.) I say *could be* with caution because ADHD is way overdiagnosed in our current culture, where the speed of life and the perpetual presence of technology keep most of us from being present. In most cases, you can be more focused by trying what I've suggested. But if it's all to no avail, and you are disorganized no matter what you do or where you are, then I recommend you call your primary care physician and ask to be referred to a specialist for an assessment.

As we conclude this chapter, I want to emphasize that maximizing your focus is absolutely nonnegotiable if you want to be successful with this book. Unless you establish authority over your digital life, begin to reduce the other distractions we went over, and apply the focus-strengthening approaches we covered, you will not have the headspace or calendar space integral to tackling the lessons on the pages ahead.

---

[7] See note 5 above.

Attorney in Action

Diego, a high-strung 30-year-old litigator, came to me for coaching because he was so on edge at work that he was making impulsive decisions and lashing out at colleagues. After introducing him to the concept of meditation with some simple exercises, I suggested that he use technology to his advantage by downloading a meditation app and trying it out before our next session. From doing just a few 10-minute guided meditations the following few weeks, he found that he was feeling less irritable, not so rushed, and more mindful in the face of disruption. Now he knows a few easy meditation techniques—closing his eyes for a minute and focusing on the in and out of his breath, for example—that he can pull out and use whenever he feels the need to corral himself back from decentering detours.

Releasing yourself from anything not aligned with exquisite self-care, a grounded perspective, nourishing diversions, and thriving relationships is pivotal to you mastering the work-plus model. This process is gradual and there is no silver bullet, but you can fast-track your progress significantly by exercising your underperforming capacity to say no. Now that you see the opportunity you didn't know existed, the key is to bring this question to every situation: *Is this getting me closer to or further from the life I want?* Whatever it is, if it's frustrating the development of a more vibrant and satisfied you, it must go.

> "Most people don't know that attentional command is their superpower. Now that you're onto that secret, nothing can stop you from zeroing in on what matters most and staying there, no matter what is happening around you."

In the spirit of dumping the extraneous, I recommend that you stick with this chapter as long as you need to be ready for a look at the next chapter, where we'll discuss habits and issues that are hindering you. We've covered a lot here, so let's remember there are no deadlines attached to this book. That means you can take however much time you need to consistently assert your restraint with technology and get at those other disruptors. You will get better results if you are brutally honest with how you are wasting your attention and then reel yourself in bit by bit, starting with the least intimidating of corrective changes and going from there. Most people don't know that attentional command is their superpower. Now that you're onto that secret, nothing can stop you from zeroing in on what matters most and staying there, no matter what is happening around you.

STAGE TWO

Regular Season

4

Gear Up

"I've never been in there," responded my attorney friend, Juliet, when I said she must be loving the amazing workout facility—complete with pool and palm trees overlooking Los Angeles—in her gorgeous condo building of two years. At that time, she was putting in 70 hours a week at a prestigious labor law firm. Still appearing as youthful as when she'd earned her black belt in karate during college, she was starting to worry about her reliance on microwaveable processed foods over wholesome meals she didn't have time to cook. Juliet didn't exercise much anymore and acknowledged that she never really felt rested. And, she had to admit, regardless of her stellar resume and enormous salary, she wasn't exactly feeling on top of the world.

"It's just part of being a lawyer," she rationalized.

Juliet's all-too-common workaholic experience underscores what attorneys don't appreciate that athletes have figured out: you must invest totally in your physical and mental health if you're going to truly succeed in a high-pressure field that claims all of you.

Yes, physical health is certainly more important to athletes than lawyers for obvious reasons, and feeling upbeat is more integral to winning an athletic competition than winning a case in court. However, prolonged peak intellectual performance is no more feasible than repeated bodily exertion without physical and psychological fitness. If you harbor that old-fashioned lawyer belief that your excellence is related solely to how well you can push yourself through work no matter how tired you are or how bad your mood is, you are mistaken. Even if you are the most

> "Even if you are the most brilliant, hardest-working, most likable attorney in town, there are limits to how far you can go if you're neglecting your fundamental needs."

brilliant, hardest-working, most likable attorney in town, there are limits to how far you can go if you're neglecting your fundamental needs. Just like Juliet (and any famous athlete whose bad habits catch up with them), you may appear to be living the good life and have everything you need, when, in fact, you are lacking the most vital substance of success.

Before we continue, let's get one thing clear:

Because they must be in superior physical and mental condition compared to everyone else, athletes take care of their bodies and brains in the most elaborate and expensive ways. They have celebrity chefs preparing meals and snacks expressly designed to deliver whatever customized eating plan will result in increased speed, agility, strength, and stamina. They have personal fitness trainers engineering them into Terminator-like, unstoppable machines. They have top-notch massage therapists, life coaches, sports psychologists, acupuncturists, you name it—all specializing in their respective athletic talent, making sure to keep them at the cutting edge of every new technique and regimen.

Please rest assured: it's not the actual extreme measures I'm advocating here but the principle of taking optimal care of yourself. Do you want to be exceptionally serious about exercise, diet, and mood? If so and you have the time and money, that is great; I say go for it, but it's not necessary. While you do have to be more mindful of your health than professionals with less taxing careers, you don't have to go all out. Follow the fundamental self-care strategies below and you will be adequately prepped to meet the above-and-beyond rigors of lawyering, day in and day out:

> "While you do have to be more mindful of your health than professionals with less taxing careers, you don't have to go all out."

LAWYER LIKE AN ATHLETE PRIMING STRATEGY #1

Get Enough Sleep

My favorite metaphor for the consequence of inadequate sleep comes from the movie *Fight Club* when Edward Norton's character explains what insomnia is like. He puts an original document through a copier, makes a copy of that copy, and a copy of that copy, and so on until all you see is an imperceptible blur. I love how W. Chris Winter, MD, sleep specialist to athletes, emphasizes the critical role of sleep in the book I recommend for sleep-challenged clients, *The Sleep Solution: Why Your Sleep Is Broken and How to Fix It*. Dr. Winter imagines the human body as a bustling big-city office building, with people dirtying things up and wearing things out as they come in and out every day. The building shuts down at night so the cleaning crew can dust off debris, sweep out rooms, and shine floors to be ready for the onslaught of the next busy day. Your body without enough sleep is like that cleaning crew not showing up.[1]

Many attorneys tell me that sleep is a waste of time because no work is getting accomplished while they're in bed, but the truth is that a great deal is happening while you're sleeping, and it's all critical to your conscious productivity. While your alert, high-level thinking brain rests, other parts of your brain are orchestrating a thorough sifting, organizing, and recalibrating process. By regularly getting enough sleep, you are ensuring that all your internal organs and systems are in top gear for whatever the next day has in store.

How much sleep it takes for that to happen is an individual thing. A small percentage of adults need only four or five hours of sleep per night, and many attorneys strive to be among those lucky people with more waking hours of the day available to them for work. The problem, unfortunately, is that you can't force yourself to thrive on less sleep than is inherent to your unique biological makeup. Most adults depend on 6 to 10 hours of sleep per night, and you know you're getting enough sleep if you wake up feeling refreshed and good to go. Anything less than that, your faculties and nerves will be frayed. Like pulling all-nighters in college and law

---

[1] W. Chris Winter MD, *The Sleep Solution: Why Your Sleep Is Broken and How to Fix It* (New York: Penguin Random House, 2017).

school, you can tough out the occasional bleary-eyed day when you're not nearly rested, but if you chronically go without enough sleep, you are giving illness a free pass to sideline you.

Now that you understand how rudimentary sleep is to the crucial "exquisite self-care" component of the work-plus model, let's take a moment to determine your sleep quota. Never mind how little sleep you *wish* you could function on; write down how many hours of sleep you *need* to be getting every night to be at your best the next day:

____

____

Now, here are some ways you can make sure you get those pivotal hours:

First, make your bedroom a sleep sanctuary. Start with a well-made, comfortable bed that supports your back and keeps you cozy. Banish anything from your bedroom that remotely revs you up, like a desk where you pay bills, a laundry basket, a television, or your laptop. Also, remove that phone you say you need on your bedside table for the alarm, because just knowing technology is within reach, giving you potential access to new texts, emails, and the internet will put your brain on alert. Once you've cleared out anything contrary to slumber, bring in whatever speaks serenity to you: calming artwork, a real clock with a light that wakes you up gradually, and colors that soothe you. Keep your bedroom dark, cool, and quiet because these are the best conditions for deep sleep.

Next, make sure you have a standard sleep schedule. Your brain likes routines and reflexes, so the overnight renewal process is most efficient when it occurs like clockwork. To institute the right schedule, determine how early you need to wake up most days, then factor in what time you need to get in bed to get in your requisite sleeping hours.

Now that you know how to set yourself up for sleep, here are some key pointers for encouraging sleep of the highest quality:

- **Establish a relaxing evening routine.** Attorneys often tell me they have trouble falling asleep because their minds are whirling when their heads hit the pillow. The thing to keep in mind here is that if you want to drift off quickly, you have to segue into sleep by winding down before bed. This amounts to shutting off your working brain about an hour before bedtime so that you can gradually let stimulating thoughts and emotions subside. You can downshift into a sleep-inducing state by putting away your phone and laptop and enjoying activities that settle you, like light reading, feel-good TV, or hot herbal tea.

- **Establish a reviving morning routine.** You will find yourself feeling less tense at the end of the day, and thereby able to fall asleep more easily, if you start your day on a positive note. This amounts to giving yourself plenty of time to get ready in the morning so that you are not raising your stress level by rushing around. Just like falling asleep, waking up is a gradual process that can't be hurried. You are most apt to be at your best when you greet the day with uncomplicated rituals like doing a few stretches, savoring your morning coffee as you peruse the news, or reading something inspiring. When you jump-start your day with pleasantly paced activities, you are more likely to feel better throughout the day, and you can slow down more readily by the time evening arrives.
- **Don't fret if you can't sleep.** Even the most committed sleep hygiene practices won't prevent you from occasionally having trouble falling or staying asleep. Sometimes you're too excited or worried about something you can pinpoint; other times there may be no rhyme or reason. The best antidote for tossing and turning is to get out of bed—because your bedroom is no place for anxiety—and do the most monotonous household chore you can conjure or read something excruciatingly boring until your eyelids start to droop. Sleeping pills are fine occasionally, like if you have trouble falling asleep while traveling on infrequent business trips, but they lose their effectiveness and can actually start keeping you awake when you rely on them too much.

> "The truth is that a great deal is happening while you're sleeping, and it's all critical to your conscious productivity."

Attorney in Action

Monica, a married mother of two who had recently launched a boutique law firm with her attorney husband, came to me for coaching because she'd gotten into a vicious cycle of drinking coffee to stay awake at work and taking sleeping pills to sleep at night. She explained that this approach had been effective initially but now was not working at all. She wasn't sleeping fully enough at night and was dragging every day despite all the caffeine. Monica's concern was that she couldn't get the rest she needed because she had to put in so many hours at work in her leadership role. I was able to convince her to come home a half-hour earlier every night so that she could improve her sleep by creating a relaxing evening routine and thus be more present as a leader in fewer working hours. By getting into a habit of winding down with the meditative rhythm of knitting, she found herself reaching for sleeping pills and coffee less, and she started feeling more alert at work just by getting the sleep she needed.

Identify one small change you can make to sleep better:

____

____

LAWYER LIKE AN ATHLETE PRIMING STRATEGY #2

Move Enough and Eat Right

You knew this strategy was coming because, just like every adult in America, you are bombarded with the message that you must eat certain foods and move your body in certain ways to be healthy. There is so much advice out there on diet and exercise, much of it inaccurate and conflicting, that you could spend the rest of your life sorting through it all.

Full disclosure here: I am not a diet and exercise expert, and so I asked competitive runner Chris LaCroix, owner of All Seasons Endurance Training, to step in. Chris is a personal trainer to many time-pressed professionals, including attorneys, and knows the essentials on this front.

Here's what Chris suggested I pass along to you (his recommendations, my words):

Just like sleep, routinely eating healthful food and sufficiently moving your body is integral to your biological processes flowing smoothly.

Sure, you can probably get by like a lot of adults eating mostly junk and being largely sedentary, but you certainly won't be anywhere near your best. Why not take the full control you have to eat and move in ways that boost your brain power, mood, confidence, motivation, longevity, and overall sense of aliveness?

> "Why not take the full control you have to eat and move in ways that boost your brain power, mood, confidence, motivation, longevity, and overall sense of aliveness?"

The great thing is you don't have to be a fanatic to get the many benefits that nutrition and physical activity bring. Even Tom Brady, known for his incredibly regimented diet, enjoys ice cream cones with his kids now and then.[2] If you're responsible with diet and exercise 80 percent of the time and eat and do whatever you please that other 20 percent, you'll be just fine. Of course, if you have an underlying medical condition, you'll need to regularly consult with your doctor on this.

Beginning with exercise, here's how you can get going with a healthy lifestyle that works for you:

Consult the experts. How much and what kind of exercise do you need? Just follow the World Health Organization (WHO; who.int) recommendation for adults. That's 150–300 minutes of moderate-intensity aerobic exercise (walking, swimming, gardening) or 75–150 minutes of vigorous-intensity physical activity (running, cycling, boxing) per week.[3]

Muscle strengthening is the other important part of exercise endorsed by the WHO, and two sessions per week is the recommendation. A combination of aerobic and weight-bearing activity helps to reduce the risk of countless medical illnesses and bodily injuries while promoting physical balance and flexibility.

---

[2] Oprah Winfrey, host, "Tom Brady: How to Reach Peak Performance," Oprah's Super Soul (podcast), June 18, 2018, accessed February 4, 2021, https://www.oprah.com/own-podcasts/tom-brady-part-1-how-to-reach-peak-performance.

[3] World Health Organization "Physical Activity," WHO, October 5, 2022, https://www.who.int/news-room/fact-sheets/detail/physical-activity.

Start slow. If you're not already athletic, work up to those WHO guidelines gradually so that you don't injure yourself or overdo it. For example, if you're sitting at a desk most of the day, you can begin by getting up and walking around for a few minutes every hour, eventually working up to a three- or four-times-per-week walking or running routine. If you're not doing any strength training right now, start with bodyweight exercises like a few push-ups or sit-ups per day, and move on to lifting actual dumbbells.

Design your exercise plan to work for you. There are endless ways to combine cardio with weight-bearing exercise, depending on your access to workout space and equipment and personal preferences. Walking, running, and bodyweight exercises can be done almost anywhere and are easiest to manage. Gyms offer all sorts of options for getting in shape, and you can do classes from home via YouTube videos and online gym offerings. It's not so much the types of exercise you choose that's important; seriously, you can mix up cardio and strength training in many different ways based on your goals. What matters most is that you stay committed to doing the program. If you want to ease the building of exercise habits that stick, a personal trainer can give you the instruction, support, and accountability to stay on course.

List one thing you can do to improve your physical fitness:

____

____

Now, let's hear what Chris conveyed to me about diet:

First, easy does it. When it comes to eating well, we often get paralyzed by the plethora of strategies out there. Do you need to start counting calories? Do you have to skip your evening glass of wine? Should you give up all processed food and go totally organic? Eating well, like exercise, is simplest when you go with the WHO's recommendations. The skinny is this: integrate fruits and vegetables into as many meals and snacks as possible; reduce fat, salt, and sugar whenever possible; and drink about 64 ounces of water per day.[4] Yes, nutrition is much more complex than this, and you

[4] World Health Organization "Healthy Diet," WHO, April 29, 2020, https://www.who.int/news-room/fact-sheets/detail/healthy-diet.

can go as far as you want on the WHO website, but working with this basic plan will point you in the right direction.

Determine where you want to intervene. To establish new and better eating habits, you need to know what's going well and what's not so that you can adapt accordingly. Keeping a food log for a few days, where you write down everything you eat, will help you to be more aware of and accurate about what you're eating throughout the day. Once you've identified some areas you can improve on—maybe you're eating candy more than you thought; perhaps what you've been calling an afternoon snack has become more of a second lunch—you can establish some sensible, healthier eating goals. The key is to decide on actions, one by one, that are the easiest to tackle with the bandwidth you have. You might substitute fruit for candy twice this week or scale back that lunch-like afternoon snack. Keep going with these modifications until you can honestly say that you eat well most of the time.

Be moderate. As you become more deliberate about what you are eating, you will make nutrition choices that make you more resilient in every way. However, you can't be perfect. Temptations to indulge ourselves with food are everywhere and almost impossible to avoid, and you won't always be able to resist. The more you constrict your eating, the more likely it is that you will rebel,

Attorney in Action

Out-of-shape corporate attorney Ryan contacted Chris for personal training after his doctor warned him that he was at high risk for heart disease. Ryan was eager to improve his health but had never been a regular exerciser and was intimidated by what he thought it might require of him. He was surprised by how little he had to do—two basic gym workouts per week—to start feeling healthier. By applying his exceptional work ethic to physical fitness, blocking exercise on his calendar as a top priority, and just arriving at the gym and following instructions, Ryan found that he was not only in better physical condition but felt more self-assured from really showing up for himself.

so, leave room in your eating plan for the inevitable, occasional slip-up (this goes for your exercise plan too.)

List one thing you can do to improve your eating:

____

____

____

LAWYER LIKE AN ATHLETE PRIMING STRATEGY #3

Address Your Issues

You're likely aware of all the athletes—John McEnroe, Abby Wambach, Kevin Love, to name a few—increasingly coming forward to admit they've had mental health challenges associated with being exceptionally driven and under intense pressure. Similar to elite athletes, attorneys generally have personality characteristics, namely perfectionism and off-the-charts ambition, that make them susceptible to becoming psychologically distressed as they endeavor to beat above-standard odds. Besides the stressors common to high-achievement careers, there are varying individual factors, such as genetics, trauma history, and personal problems, that can make mental illness more likely. It's not a matter of whether or not you have issues, because, frankly, we all have issues. It's more a question of whether you have particular issues that are making your career and life more complicated than they have to be.

"It's not a matter of whether or not you have issues, because, frankly, we all have issues. It's more a question of whether you have particular issues that are making your career and life more complicated than they have to be."

So, how do you know if there's something you should take a deeper look at?

It's tricky to distinguish between the regular hardcore stress of lawyering and signs of a fundamental internal condition because the manifestations can be so similar. Here's how to know you're in need of professional intervention:

You can't snap out of it. Ups and downs are a normal part of adulthood. We all have bad moments and bad days due to the inescapable frustrations, disappointments, and losses inherent in work and life. A good indicator that psychological distress is more than just an everyday reaction is that it doesn't subside no matter what you do to cheer yourself up or calm yourself down. A reliable rule of thumb is that if you're consistently feeling depressed, anxious, or otherwise out of sorts for two weeks or longer, it's wise to get counsel, especially if you haven't undergone an identifiable trigger like a recent life change or loss.

It's getting in your way. There are as many psychological theories as there are psychologists, but one thing most of us agree on is that an issue needs addressing if it's interfering with your ability to effectively participate in the basic responsibilities of adulthood. This means that if your thoughts and moods are negatively impacting your work, relationships with others, or relationship with yourself, then you may want to seek out a professional. On the other hand, if the only internal roadblock you can think of is an intense snake phobia and you live in Manhattan, it's probably okay to not seek treatment.

You detect a pattern. One more narrowing-down rule psychologists see eye to eye on is that an issue is most likely an issue if it is part of a destructive cycle in your life. If you've noticed, for example, that you always seem to become romantically involved with partners who cheat on you, that you seem to get fired more than most people you know, or that your family and friends complain to you about the same habit or trait, then there is most likely some inner matter making trouble for you. Similarly, if you suspect that certain ingrained beliefs—*I must always win! If I am not perfect, I am not okay! I don't deserve what I want*—are blocking your growth, therapy could help. It's hard to see patterns in ourselves, so you might want to ask a close confidant if you're missing anything.

It's back again! Something else psychologists agree on is that important lessons not learned will circle around until they get your attention. A basic tenet of psychological health is that if a person accomplishes the tasks of the developmental stage they're in, be it toilet training, leaving the nest, or managing a budget, they will be fully equipped for the next stage. If they fail to master the tasks of a certain stage, they move forward unable to handle the increasingly complex challenges of life. Whatever you don't overcome, in other words, you take with you to your next destination, and that's where psychological baggage can get heavy. So, if you think your peers have mastered a life lesson you're still grappling with, it makes sense to take time out for some therapeutic tutoring.

You are self-medicating. It's perfectly fine (if it's been approved by your medical doctor) to let loose occasionally: drinking, eating, or partaking in legal recreational drugs to celebrate or decompress. After all, escapism can help to even out your self-discipline, reward all your hard work, and send you back to your good habits feeling renewed. However, if you're routinely imbibing to suppress difficult emotions, numb yourself from unreckoned memories, or fill yourself with a sense of warmth or courage, you should be wary. When you rely on transitory substances to cope rather than responsibly attack the problem, you start to lose faith in your own power to get through tough times; and when you see the spiral of substances providing temporary relief, but then catapulting you right back to where you started, a little deeper each time, you become more and more stuck. The best thing to do if you think you might have a substance abuse problem (or any kind of psychological condition) is to contact your state lawyer assistance program. The fact that your profession has its own starting point for substance abuse and mental health intervention tells you that self-medication is rampant and ruinous in the legal field. No matter where you are on that path, it's never too late to reverse the damage.

"The best thing to do if you think you might have a substance abuse problem (or any kind of psychological condition) is to contact your state lawyer assistance program."

So, was all that a little humbling? I'm hoping so.

However, regardless of where you are with all the self-care strategies we just went over, you can start turning things around. The ultimate goal is to lawyer like an athlete. The only prerequisite is that you begin abolishing anything unduly depleting the mental, emotional, and physical resources for this expedition.

Attorney in Action

Nicco, a hotshot young attorney celebrated for moving up at his firm with meteoric speed, came for coaching with me because he didn't feel successful despite the evidence of success all around him. He realized that he was worn out from trying futilely for most of his life to do something that would finally make his parents proud. Nothing—skipping an elementary school grade, making high school high honor roll, earning an Ivy League scholarship, or even winning a major election—had ever been good enough to earn their validation. Through our conversations, Nicco was able to see that pleasing himself was more important than pleasing his parents, which was a goal he could actually reach. By repeatedly recognizing his parents' impossible standards when they arose in his head and replacing them with his own, more reasonable metrics of success, Nicco started to feel as accomplished as he deserved to feel.

You have finished the preparation part of this book, and you now know you have more agency over your life than you thought—*if* you're willing to put more into yourself. You understand the work-plus model, you get that the tiny-step method is the way to go, you see your responsibility in creating opportunities for yourself, and you know what you can do, mind, body, and soul, to arrive at a happier and more productive existence. Now, with a full understanding of what you are getting into, you are ready to build on what you've started with another level of learning and doing. As always, spend as much time as you need on the chapter you're in, integrating and experimenting at your own pace, and only move on when you feel you've turned principle into practice.

"You have finished the preparation part of this book, and you now know you have more agency over your life than you thought—*if* you're willing to put more into yourself."

5

Optimize Your Optimism

Celebrity athletes are adored by many. We look up to them because we assume their rock-star status gives them access to the best that life has to offer. We are so certain, without even knowing them, that their lives are better than ours that we aspire to be like them and are envious of all the trappings—enormous talent, charisma, wealth, connections—we're sure are the ticket to what we call the good life.

However, we don't consider in this limited model of success the other side of that glorified persona. Think of the pressure to live up to how your fans perceive you and what they expect of you when that image is superhuman, unrealistic, and not true to who you really are, especially in a culture that vilifies celebrities for making minor mistakes. Consider the disappointment of always traveling to exotic places and not having the space outside your training, performance, and media appearance schedule to explore them. And yes, star athletes get exceptionally privileged and sought-after invitations, but they don't have time away from their rigorous work to say yes to more than a fraction of those opportunities. Add on the slog of being on the road, away from family most days of the year, and the need to always know what your competitors are doing so that you can stay one step ahead of the game.

Being a sports champion is not as appealing as it looks. Just like the staggering social position, the stressors are outsized too. Perpetually coming at them are bigger-than-average struggles that can make the glass seem half-empty, and so it's pretty easy to give up.

The most successful athletes realize early on that they can't afford the drag of a half-empty perspective. The athletes you see at the top, those who make it through all the stultifying hurdles, get there by adopting a glass-half-full perspective that bats away noise, then homes in on valid problems and swiftly addresses them. The real pros know how to navigate through hardship without getting mired in it, which prevents the squelching of energy from an overly negative focus. As health podcaster Mark Steele puts it, "Successful athletes find direction through the garbage by using positivity as a road map."[1]

A perfect example of this kind of approach is Tom Brady being told when he was starting out that he didn't have the physical talent to be a football pro. A lot of athletes would've stopped at that blow, but Brady chose instead to succeed by putting his efforts into what he *did* have going for him: an unwavering passion to go beyond standard training to maximize his physical potential.[2] Brady's knack for being undeterred by naysayers and his commitment to being the best he can be is what powers every team he joins. His ability to take punches ("Tom, you're not fast enough!" "Tom, you don't know how to run!"), consider them, and then find resonant alternative paths forward is what distinguishes him. Rather than get bummed out by his weak points, he compensates with his exceptional throwing arm and phenomenal strategic thinking . . . and that's the kind of secret sauce that wins Super Bowls.

What Tom Brady and a lot of other star athletes have mastered is referred to by psychologists as the solution-focused approach. Solution-focused therapists help their clients get unhooked from being stuck by tamping down on complaining and maximizing positive movement. Solution-focused therapy can be transformative in just 8 to 10 sessions because it teaches the pragmatic skills needed to not get

> "The primary benefit of being solution-focused is a healthy intolerance for situations that slow your progress to be the best, so you feel freer, more rewarded, and more confident."

[1] Mark Steele, host, "Positivity for Professional Athletes," Your Life Depends On It (podcast), November 3, 2020.

[2] Oprah Winfrey, host, "Tom Brady: How to Reach Peak Performance," Oprah's Super Soul (podcast), June 18, 2018, accessed February 4, 2021, https://www.oprah.com/own-podcasts/tom-brady-part-1-how-to-reach-peak-performance.

unnecessarily weighed down by the inexorable trials of life and work. The primary benefit of this approach is a healthy intolerance for situations that slow your progress to be the best, so you feel freer, more compensated, and more confident.

For an attorney, a solution-focused approach is integral to success. You can't possibly lawyer like an athlete if you are being unduly drained in any way of enthusiasm, belief, or tenacity. You need to regularly take a step back from your work and life to fully see what is going on, and take immediate responsibility for removing any obstacle under your control. You need to be majorly sophisticated at spotting and squelching deterrents to your embracing the work-plus model—because those missiles will keep coming at you whether you like it or not. To get good at this, you must look seriously at the outwardly oppositional circumstances you encounter—critical feedback about your performance, attacks on your character, accusatory clients—extract what you can improve upon, and then act on a proactive course forward. By examining what's hard to hear like athletes do and looking for kernels of truth that are worth working on, you'll eventually develop the solution-focused steeliness to counter the law world's outsized, potentially derailing asks.

Attorney in Action

Magdalena, a second-year associate, sought coaching to determine if she really had the right constitution for being an attorney. She liked the work, but negative feedback about her performance ("You're not assertive enough." "You don't speak up enough.") had her wondering if she should switch careers. I suggested that Magdalena was being influenced by the generalization that the best attorneys are aggressive and insistent; could it be that she could be successful as an unassuming introvert? Could she shine in other, more productive ways than lining up with typecasting? By looking more deeply at criticism, letting only valid reasons stop her, and finding ways to shine that aligned with her nature, she was able to feel more comfortable in her position. Sure, she still took criticism seriously, acknowledging, for example, that she needed to get better at being vocal at meetings and getting heard, then taking tiny steps—vowing to speak up at least once at every meeting and going from there—to maximize her voice. But she learned to toss out the irrelevant aspects of commentary that provided no value and only got in her way.

"That fight-flight age is long gone, our threats are less immediate, and the overemphasis on what's not good keeps us from capitalizing on what *is* good."

Before you take on this challenge, understand that the forward thinking I'm advocating is underdeveloped in humans, and it's going to take consistent effort. All of us are stubbornly hardwired to notice problems over solutions and prioritize the negative over the positive, for survival reasons. It made sense at the beginning of civilization for us to be hyperaware of saber-toothed tigers, poisonous plants, and all manner of primitive hazards lurking about; if you looked away even for a minute, you could get wiped out. But that fight-flight age is long gone, our threats are less immediate, and the overemphasis on what's not good keeps us from capitalizing on what *is* good.

My point here is that optimizing your optimism means you're going to have to relearn how you think. We'll begin that process in this chapter and go more fully into modifying your mindset in the chapters ahead.

Self-help books tell us that we can avoid the inevitable pain of being human by drowning out the negative with positive affirmations: *I can do whatever I want. I deserve the finest of everything. I am unbeatable (even if I have glaring issues and don't like myself very much).* Famous people with chronic diseases tell us that we can avoid suffering by just "deciding" to be happy. Motivational speakers assure us that we can accomplish whatever we want by simply going over and over our desired positive outcomes in our heads. What we take away from all this "positive-thinking" hype is that force-feeding ourselves happy thoughts will bulldoze us over insecurity, doubt, fear, sadness, grief, and every other inconvenient psychological experience and coax us toward eternal bliss. While all these tools can help, the fact is that a fundamental change in outlook is essential, beginning with a solution-focused foundation.

Optimism is a courageous discipline that prospers over time as clear-sightedness steadily takes hold over wishful thinking. It's not about denying reality, telling yourself everything is fine when it's not, pushing down uncomfortable emotions, or plastering a perpetual smile on your face. The capacity to look at life squarely, acknowledge what you're dealing with, and make it your mission to work with, rather than resist or regret, whatever situation is before you is an art that requires daily intention and dedication.

There's no getting through life as a human being without disappointments, failures, losses, condemnations, and all sorts of other hindrances and unexpected disasters, but optimism certainly makes trials and tribulations easier to bear and maneuver around.

> "Optimism is a courageous discipline that prospers over time as clear-sightedness steadily takes hold over wishful thinking."

No matter where you are currently on the optimism scale—overly optimistic to the point where you miss important information, so pessimistic that you see only doom and gloom, or somewhere in between—solution-focused thinking is no-nonsense hard work.

The best reason for doing the work?

The payoff of being an optimistic problem-solver is that positivity attracts positivity, meaning that big breaks come much more readily when you are looking up instead of down.

> "The payoff of being an optimistic problem-solver is that positivity attracts positivity, meaning that big breaks come much more readily when you are looking up instead of down."

Have you noticed that attorneys who complain incessantly, blame everyone but themselves for their troubles, and seem to be forever in crisis just bring on more of the same? Just like the most successful athletes, attorneys are more likely to attract good fortune when they limit their griping, access their own personal power for positive change, and then make the most of what they already have right now.

That's optimism in a nutshell.

Here are some strategies you can employ to start optimizing your optimism:

Notice positive moments. You can feel steadily more hopeful by simply striving to see what's going well in your life. While landing a new client or paying off a loan counts, it's the little things you're probably missing that matter most here, like noticing when someone happens to smile at you or open a door for you as you go

Attorney in Action

Frederic sought my coaching because he felt too beleaguered by pressing marital and money issues to bring a positive attitude to his work. Every day seemed darker and drearier as he became more convinced that he wouldn't ever be able to get things right, and the belief that it would take a major turn of events to improve his outlook only added to his despondency. Totally doubtful at first that it would work, Frederic agreed to try on a "what have I got to lose?" mindset. He began to notice a few little things every day—hearing from a friend he hadn't talked to in a while, not forgetting his umbrella on a rainy afternoon, a pleasing piece of mail amid the usual past-due bills—that were signs of light for him, and he wrote them down. Two sessions later, he seemed a little brighter as he recounted with incredulousness about how he simply observed and documented such seemingly minute entries: pastry was extra tasty this morning; there was a pretty cool cardinal outside my window; that asshole attorney made a funny joke. He began to open his mind and see problem-solving opportunities as his positive moments added up, and his ever-expanding solution focus eventually got him on top of and able to resolve his relationship and financial concerns.

about your day, observing the clear sky above you and the fresh air around you when you're walking from one place to the next, or fully savoring the aroma of your morning coffee or a blossoming bush in spring. Being purposefully open to what delights you will increasingly weaken that all-too-human reflex to turn toward what's not so enjoyable. (Before the skeptical side of you does an eye roll here, consider that even the tiniest bit of gratitude boosts your mood and opens your mind, thereby encouraging the motivated, grounded-in-reality problem-solving state you're after.)

List three positive moments you experience over the next day or so:

1. ______________________________
2. ______________________________
3. ______________________________

End on a positive note. It's a natural instinct to recall each day according to what went wrong, and noting that you didn't accomplish something or were criticized can dampen your evening. You can exercise optimism by instead recalling three things that went well. Again, start with the small things that you've probably been dismissing. Maybe you can say that today you managed to take that bullying judge less personally, you drank more water than usual, or you found time for a reviving break.

At the end of today, list three things that went well for you:

1. ______________________________
2. ______________________________
3. ______________________________

(Suggestion: it's not necessary, but I recommend that you document positive moments as they happen by jotting down your three daily things that go well in a journal or notebook or speaking them into your phone. When you put positive thoughts to paper or device, they tend to have more of an impact on brightening your outlook; also, you'll develop an ever-growing record of optimism that you can look back on when you need some reminding.)

If you're eye-rolling again, I'm not telling you to drink Kool-Aid or look at the world with rose-colored glasses. I admit that in our bad-news-obsessed culture, it seems pretty weird to swivel over to what's going right on even the cloudiest days. Remember: you are not wired to think this way. It takes a real determination to upend an entrenched global leaning and think for yourself, and though you may hope it's possible to be appreciative and also keep your feet on the ground, it will take real-life evidence to believe you won't topple from positive thinking.

Embrace what is. Think of an area of your life you want to improve in some major way. Maybe you have exceeded your job or house and can't see a clear path to the next step. Find a way to make your current circumstances more satisfying, and see what happens. You might make a list of what you *do* like about your current job or house and decide to be more fully engaged with what you already have at hand. By extracting optimism from the present, you will likely bring on remedies and routes you hadn't considered.

List one life or work factor you want to improve:

____

____

Find the problem in the solution. Think of a problem you're dealing with currently, something you're really battling with. Ask yourself what opportunities are hiding in this trying situation. Maybe a difficult person is helping you to become more patient. Perhaps unemployment is allowing you extra time to pursue a hobby you had put on the back burner. Consider intriguing pathways or possibilities you hadn't noticed or appreciated before. When you're hard-pressed to notice roses amid the thorns, ask a mentor what gift you're not seeing.

List one problem in your life:

____

____

What are the positives you see within that problem?

____

____

Attorney in Action

Wren, single and in her 30s, came to coaching in a serious rut. She was doing fairly well career-wise but wasn't able to afford a bigger home or find the right life partner. She found herself wanting to get out of her current home whenever possible because she was so tired of it, and worried that she'd end up alone for the rest of her life. I asked her to consider that her negative assessment of and restlessness in her current personal life could be dampening her mood unnecessarily and possibly slowing down her progress. Rather than dwell on what she didn't have, I suggested she could improve her outlook simply by finding new ways to revel in the benefits she already had. Just by buying some new throw pillows that she loved, she changed the way she felt about her house. By listing all the flexibility she had as an unattached woman, she was able to appreciate her singledom more fully. Wren began to realize the benefits of rooting out the positive, namely a more accepting and encouraging perspective, that seemed magnetic to better and better opportunities. The more she created space for new options, the more she was able to grow at work, too, building better legal arguments and finding unexpected routes around objections.

After you've opted for optimism for a week or two, stop and consider what you're experiencing. Are you sensing your mind opening up? Do you notice anything becoming easier or feeling lighter? Are ideas, insights, and answers coming more readily? What are you attracting?

"As you continue to evolve your optimism, letting go more and more of that negative grip, you will increasingly be propelled rather than compromised by complications."

The best part of practicing positivity is that it has an enormous influence on how your life plays out around you. As you continue to evolve your optimism, letting go more and more of that negative grip, you will increasingly be propelled rather than compromised by complications. As you keep refining your solution focus, you'll see greater and greater proof that your optimism is resulting in improved circumstances at work and at home. Soak in the way Olympic runner Deena Kastor explains it in her memoir chronicling the incredible power of her mentality in transforming her career: "A good attitude goes far beyond the general idea of staying positive. It is part of a discipline, a long-cultivated habit of building and sustaining a positive mind capable of turning every experience into fuel."[3]

The next chapter will move you further into the grounded perspective part of the work-plus model, beyond this introductory overview into refining your solution focus to make it lawyer-specific. You've learned through the earlier chapters that you have way more control than you thought over your life. As you'll see in the pages ahead, that sense of command, be it at a rock-bottom low or impossible high, is proportional to and powered by the stance you take.

One more thing to mull over as we conclude this chapter:

You think for a living, and now you're working on improving your thinking. That's a lot to ask of your already high-functioning brain. Before you continue with more of what psychologists call cognitive restructuring, please give your brain a deserved and needed break. To finish this chapter feeling recharged and refreshed, pause to engage in mindless frivolity for at least one hour. No matter how serious you are about changing your thinking, you can't be genuinely or generally positive if you're not enjoying yourself.

---

[3] Deena Kastor and Michelle Hamilton, *Let Your Mind Run: A Memoir of Thinking My Way to Victory* (New York: Crown Publishing, 2018), 3.

6

Condition Your Thoughts

Sarah, a Florida immigration attorney with her own practice and half-custody of two teenagers, arrives her standard 10 minutes late to our online coaching session with damp hair and a bowl of cereal. She laments while eating her breakfast about her crazy morning routine, snowballing workload, endless court delays, and frantic clients who blame her for the bureaucracy she is exhausted from fighting. "All I think about is that I'm not cut out for this," she says with utter exasperation, "I try looking at the silver lining to stay motivated, but nothing is working. Negative thoughts keep popping up."

As I do with all the attorneys—and there are a lot of them—who come to me wondering why they can't sustain a positive attitude in the face of tremendous, unrelenting stress, I say to Sarah, "To lawyer like an athlete, you must tend to your thoughts like an athlete." And then I ask her, "Have you heard of Naomi Osaka?"

I explain to Sarah that Osaka, though she has reached the pinnacle of physical shape and is one of the best tennis players in the world, struggles with intrusive internal chatter that can get in the way of her game. I cite Naomi's recent openness about familiar, self-defeating thoughts that flare up under pressure: "I must win every time, or I am a failure; my support team will never forgive me if I make a mistake; I will not recover if I say the wrong thing to the press."[1] And I tell Sarah that it's not just Naomi; even the most optimistic athletes experience unwelcome thoughts that

[1] *Naomi Osaka*, directed by Garrett Bradley (Netflix Series, 2021), https://www.netflix.com/title/81128594.

can interfere with performance because it's human nature for thoughts to course untethered through our minds all day long. They range from "I ate too much last night" to "I don't like the lighting in here" to "I need to pick up the dry-cleaning" to "I can't do this." I emphasize that reducing the pull of that never-ending, all-too-human inner dialogue is a critical, ongoing process for Olympian athletes as well as high-performing attorneys. As legendary golfer Jack Nicklaus aptly put it, "Your mind should always be your strongest weapon in your game."[2]

Beyond having the can-do attitude we talked about in the last chapter, star athletes need the conscientious construction of a mindset that attracts productive thoughts and neutralizes any negative ones, however small, that might stifle performance. Thoughts, haphazard by nature, can never be controlled; however, they can be influenced by a customized overall outlook that reduces mental clutter.

Creating a muscular mental framework capable of taming and shaping inner chatter is not nearly as simplistic as just saying positive statements to yourself in front of your mirror every morning or taking up meditation. Affirming yourself is a useful way to boost confidence, and meditation, as we've discussed, is a wonderful practice for calming the mind and taking irrelevant inner talk less seriously. However, neither of these popular mindfulness techniques is enough. To lawyer like an athlete, a total shift in one's basic approach to thinking is integral, and this requires disciplined dedication and the full clarity that, in the fitting words of basketball legend Kareem Abdul-Jabbar, "Your mind is what makes everything else work."[3]

Athletes must seriously alter their inner world to prevent random thoughts—often innocuous, sometimes self-defeating, usually irritating—from even slightly slowing them down, jostling their mood, or interfering with their focus. It's about learning to ignore the noise inside your head so that you can concentrate on what's most critical.

Likewise, attorneys need to keep their minds on what they need to accomplish without being sidetracked by toxic self-talk. It's a tough, day-in-and-day-out, never-ending lifestyle commitment—as opposed to a

---

[2] Steven Ungerleider, *Mental Training for Peak Performance: Top Athletes Reveal the Mind Exercises They Use to Excel* (Pennsylvania: Rodale Press, 2005), 116.

[3] Jim Afremow, *The Champion's Mind: How Great Athletes Think, Train, and Thrive* (Pennsylvania: Rodale Press, 2013), 5.

Attorney in Action

Pete, a seasoned attorney at a big city firm, believed he couldn't refuse any client request and was beyond overworked and exhausted. Running through his head all day were stressful thoughts like "I can't say no," "It's not okay to take breaks," "I don't have time for a life." With persistent practice, he created a more reasonable conviction that setting boundaries produces better results. Now Pete's thoughts are along the lines of "Saying yes only to what I have room for is smart," "Taking care of myself makes me a better attorney," "I am more efficient when I regularly relax my brain." He is performing better, his clients are happier, and he feels increasingly energized, motivated, and engaged in every area of life.

crash-diet type of approach—to generate a mostly fortifying, rather than rattling, thought train. Through the hundreds of clients I've worked with as I've developed my *Lawyer Like an Athlete* program during the past several years, I've witnessed that the undertaking is well worth it.

When you make it your daily intention to integrate the six following principles used by high-profile athletes, you will acquire a confidence-reinforcing, focus-enhancing, stamina-solidifying cognitive proficiency. The more deeply rooted these concepts become in your psyche, the more reflexive they will be in the face of those involuntary thoughts that can knock the less resilient off course.

Here are the principles:

LAWYER LIKE AN ATHLETE THOUGHT-CONDITIONING PRINCIPLE #1

Take Your Stressful Thoughts to Court

Do you recall thinking you'd never recover after getting dumped, failing an important test, or losing a job? Do you remember thinking you'd always be set after being chosen by an esteemed academic program, landing a big promotion, or having a house offer accepted? When you look back at those low and high points and the exaggerated thoughts they triggered, you see that any situation that is particularly upsetting or uplifting is likely to bring on all-or-nothing conclusions that aren't necessarily aligned with what's really happening.

It's not just the major life events that cause thinking to be out of whack with reality; our thoughts can yank us too far up or too far down throughout every day. An email subject line tells you time is running out to register for an event, and your first thought is that you'll get left behind if you don't act now—and then you're frazzled the rest of the afternoon. An unexpectedly smooth interaction with a typically prickly colleague prompts the thought that everything is now fine with this person, and you let down your guard prematurely. Whether off-base thoughts lead you to feel overly worked up or too confident, you are likely to be unnecessarily deflected, miss important details, and not be ready whenever work or life confounds you. You can be more relaxed and realistic about the good times and the bad when you manage your mind's reactivity.

Our thoughts tend to be most extreme, and thus most destabilizing, when we are caught off guard by surprising circumstances. The more you are living in your own head rather than the real world, the harder the fall when reality hits. An overly idealistic athlete expecting always to win is likely to be more distraught over a loss than a teammate who fully embraces the truth that loss is unavoidable in an extraordinarily competitive career. Because seasoned athletes understand that doggedness, self-discipline, and doubts are part of the job, they are not flustered when things don't go their way. They expect disappointments, so they don't feel demoralized by the inevitable letdowns. Likewise, the best athletes don't feel invincible when they win. They understand that there will never be a point when they don't have to work at keeping their edge. They know that when they're striving for rewards that require Herculean prowess, there will be periods of disappointment and reentry. Similarly, they don't get too comfortable or too carried away with success; they celebrate well-earned accomplishments and get back to work. Paralympic swimming gold medalist Jessica Long rounds out the ebb and flow by telling herself, "At the end of the day, it's just swimming."[4]

The challenge is comparable for attorneys. If you don't want to waste time and energy bouncing back from demoralizing disappointments and coming down to earth from grandiose highs that puff you up, you need to keep your career expectations reasonable. When you embrace mistakes and failures as part of success in a cutthroat field, you can frame forgetting

---

[4] Maggie Ryan, "Jessica Long Has 29 Paralympic Medals, but She Knows Swimming 'Doesn't Define Me as a Person,'" *Popsugar*, September 13, 2021, https://www.popsugar.com/fitness/jessica-long-talks-2021-paralympics-mental-health-48500167.

to file something important or losing a case not as catastrophic but as inevitable missteps that motivate you to do better next time. Likewise, when you recognize particularly satisfying moments as occasional payoffs for your hard work, you will be less likely to get a big head if you crush it in front of an intimidating judge or bring in a coveted client.

When you brace yourself for the worst and the best of lawyering, your thoughts will be less disruptive when curveballs and triumphs come your way. So, if you don't get made partner, think "I'm not ready yet so I'll need to get more experience" instead of the far more stressful "I'm never going to be good enough." Likewise, if you're honored in some way, think "This acknowledgment is gratifying" rather than the potentially costly "I've made it and I can just coast now." The more sound your appraisal of yourself and what you're up against is, the less jarring your thoughts will be, and the more easily you'll be able to reestablish your resolve when you are surprised by events that don't go as planned.

FIELD-TEST TAKING YOUR STRESSFUL THOUGHTS TO COURT HERE:

List a thought that is causing you stress:

____

____

____

Now, list evidence against this stressful thought: (For example, if you listed the thought "I'm never going to make that deadline" as the cause of your stress, evidence against that could be "I thought I'd never get through that first year of law school and I did it; I've reached ridiculous deadlines before.")

____

____

____

Based on your evidence, list a more motivating thought: (You might arrive at "I can do all this work if I take it one tiny step at a time.")

____

____

____

Attorney in Action

Environmental law attorney Emily used to judge herself harshly—"I'm an idiot, I've totally messed this up"—for making occasional typos when writing up documents, and her stress level would skyrocket from an associated sense of inferiority and hopelessness. Now when she's feeling unduly stressed, she knows to look at her thoughts and adjust them—"I made an error but it's no big deal; lawyers make corrections all the time"—to dial her anxiety down. The more she notices, stops, and fine-tunes her mental reactions, the fewer mistakes she makes and the calmer and more capable she feels.

LAWYER LIKE AN ATHLETE THOUGHT-CONDITIONING PRINCIPLE #2

Embrace Exceptions to Your Unwritten Rules

The main reason our thoughts have such reign over us, hijacking our peace of mind, is that we so readily believe them without question. The critical thing to get here is it's usually your thoughts about the situation rather than the actual situation that take your power away.

Remember, those thoughts perpetually cruising around in your head on their own accord are random and often based on conjured-up probabilities rather than the unpredictability of real life. For an athlete, this could mean looking forward to scoring big after investing in the best coach money can buy—and then getting angry when they lose because that miracle coach was supposed to be insurance against loss. For you, this might come down to counting on a routine court proceeding ending by a certain time because that's how it usually goes—and then becoming impatient and annoyed when the day drags on. You can waste much time and energy rebounding from the upset created by things not going exactly how you expected them to during an average day. When you prepare to do your best, factoring in that life is about constant change with no guarantees, you are better able to deal with situations that don't transpire according to the wishes in your head.

You can challenge those assumptions. By adamantly unpacking your "in a perfect world" theories and converting them to hypotheses—"Things normally go efficiently when I'm organized, but sometimes roadblocks can happen"—you will develop a general belief that will always pull you through: "There's no telling what will unfold in an unpredictable world, but whatever happens, I can figure out how to handle it." When you elasticize the laws you've arbitrarily constructed, your happiness and success are less contingent on getting your needs and wants met in specific ways, and you can be more present and at ease with what is happening around you. You are also likely to experience the upside of unpredictability: pleasant surprises.

FIELD-TEST REFINING YOUR UNWRITTEN RULES HERE:

As you move through your week, notice how you may get stressed by situations that mess with your well-laid plans. For example, there's a long line at the grocery store where you don't usually encounter lines, an uncooperative customer service person overcomplicates a simple transaction, or a tech snafu throws your morning off.

Now, write below any hard-fast assumptions causing your stress (such as "A half-hour is plenty of time to get groceries." "People want to be helpful." "Planning ensures that I meet my deadlines.")

____

____

____

Attorney in Action

New family law associate Oliver went into client meetings expecting to run through his well-organized agendas in a streamlined way. He prided himself on being an excellent time manager who could keep things on schedule. He'd become agitated when some clients, overwhelmed with emotion, would cause him to veer off his agenda. When Oliver adapted his meeting formula to account for responses from others, he was able to accommodate varying client reactions without getting stressed. Now he is more relaxed and centered at meetings, trusting that he can dovetail as needed and still manage a meeting skillfully.

Next, upgrade those assumptions to allow for the uncontrollable, thereby scaling stress way back. (For example: "Errands are usually quick, but sometimes there are unforeseen complications." "Most people want to be helpful, but some people can make things harder." "Agendas are useful but disruptions can interfere.")

Write your upgraded assumptions here:

____

____

____

LAWYER LIKE AN ATHLETE THOUGHT-CONDITIONING PRINCIPLE #3

Pivot Toward Possibility

We've established that jarring random thoughts can quickly gain momentum in a negative direction, often leading us to unnecessarily upsetting, worst-case scenarios that may never happen. Another effective method for defusing disruptive thoughts is to corral them and push them toward a more encouraging route. Athletes do this by capturing upsetting automatic thoughts and reframing them as statements and questions that open up rather than shut down opportunity.

Probably the best example of turning a train of thought around is when Magic Johnson, after being diagnosed with HIV at a time when AIDS was fatal, went from "This is the end for me" to "I'm going to beat this and have fun."[5] As another example, an athlete sidelined by an injury might pivot from "What will happen to me if I can't recover from this?" to the much more empowering question: "How can I best heal from this injury and play even better?" An athlete threatened by the competition might shift from "If we lose, we're not going to make it to the playoffs" to "If I play my best today, I can up our chances."

Attorneys can do this too. When you're feeling completely inundated with work, pivot from "How will I ever get this done?" to "How would an attorney I really respect approach this challenge?" or shift from "I never do well with that hostile attorney" to "I'm pretty good at getting along with people."

---

[5] Deseret News, "'I'm Going To Beat It,' Magic Tells the World," *Deseret News*, November 8, 1991, https://www.deseret.com/1991/11/8/18950432/i-m-going-to-beat-it-magic-tells-the-world.

The important thing here is to recognize that any distracting statements or questions—from "The air in here isn't very fresh" to "Why is this happening to me?"—can start a self-defeating train of thought capable of sabotaging performance. When you are intentional every day at intervening before a potentially destructive train of thought can take hold, empowering automatic thoughts will become more the norm.

FIELD-TEST PIVOTING TOWARD POSSIBILITY HERE:

Recall some of the negative automatic thoughts that go through your head under high stress, and list them here:

Now, write positive statements and questions that can stimulate a more productive train of thought. Remember, focus on what you can do, not what you can't do; what can go right, not what can go wrong. (For example, you might go from "This job is brutal" to "What can I do to make this easier?")

Write another negative self-talk statement here:

Now write another positive pivot here: (You might pivot from "I'm not going to win this" to "This is a good challenge, I'm going to focus on bringing the best I've got this.")

Attorney in Action

Aaron, a highly respected partner at a large law firm, was completely thrown when three of his best associates resigned in the same week—all for different reasons not due to him. He tossed and turned at night wondering what he'd done to drive his great team away and how he'd get along without them. Then he began to ask himself more productive questions: "How can I look at this as an opportunity to create an even better team? What strengths can I apply to attract top candidates? How can I collaborate with my partners to ease this transition?" When he pivoted from self-blame and fear of change to a curious, adventurous outlook, Aaron got excited about new possibilities.

LAWYER LIKE AN ATHLETE THOUGHT-CONDITIONING PRINCIPLE #4

Strive for a Fan's Perspective

Athletes commonly learn to treat themselves with the same unwavering support that their biggest fans show them. They are buoyed during episodes of self-doubt and performance anxiety, intolerance for their imperfections, and impatience with the grind by knowing that their fans fully believe in their value and potential and have reasonable expectations of them. The classic figure skater Dorothy Hamill, for example, used to think of the steadfast admiration of her proud family and friends to get herself through slippery thoughts on the ice. Research shows that when athletes talk themselves through tricky moments from a third-person fan's perspective, they feel an added dose of encouragement that can only come from calling up steady sources of support. For example: "*You've* got this" instead of "*I've* got this;" "*We* know you can do this" versus "*I* know I can do this."[6]

Attorneys can stay heartened in this same way by thinking about who their fan base is: friends, family, colleagues. When you're questioning yourself professionally or struggling to sustain your momentum, maybe facing an accelerated deadline when you're running on empty, ask yourself whether your biggest fans would agree with whatever self-defeating thoughts might be coming up. Then start reminding yourself what they'd

[6] Dorothy Hamill.

probably be saying to you: "You're a pro and you can totally figure this out; you're going to make this happen!"

When you're under the gun, remember that your fans are there to catch you when you fall, and they don't expect you to be perfect. Seeing yourself as your fans see you—a person to be cheered on and celebrated—will also keep at the forefront the importance of taking time away from work, recovering from setbacks, basking in your achievements with those you love, and generally treating yourself well so that you can stay in the game.

FIELD-TEST STRIVING FOR A FAN PERSPECTIVE HERE:

List your biggest fans, those who treasure and believe in you most, here: (Think family, friends, colleagues, mentors, community members, pets)

____

____

____

Now list some motivating phrases from your fan base that could cheer you on: (A childhood friend might say, "I've known you my whole life, and I know what you're made of." A mentor might say, "Mistakes are a sign that you are learning and growing.")

____

____

____

Attorney in Action

Asian attorney Brian was nervous about litigating a case out of town, which meant staying at a hotel for two weeks and dealing with an unfamiliar courtroom in a nondiverse area. He wasn't sure he could keep his confidence up without the everyday sources of support he had at home. Brian's solution was to call up an encouraging Chinese phrase his grandmother used to say to him to ease his anxiety. By writing the phrase down and reading it over and over, he felt encouraged during his trip and was able to fully direct his attention to doing a great job.

LAWYER LIKE AN ATHLETE THOUGHT-CONDITIONING PRINCIPLE #5

Take the Long View

Every standout professional sports career is a series of wins and losses, setbacks and recoveries, twists and turns. No famous athlete is as good as their best day or as bad as their worst, but a culmination of varying performances ultimately trending upward. Wise to this truth at a young age, Muhammad Ali reassured his fans after his first major defeat—a huge shock following a seemingly never-ending series of victories: "This is just one loss."[7]

Attorneys, like athletes, need to adopt this view of success as a general pattern of achievement over time, with inevitable dips mixed in, to keep a grounded, steady outlook. This applies to unproductive client meetings, poor performance reviews, lost cases, unforeseen hold-ups, and any other normal disappointments in the world of law as par for an extended course and not a way to gauge progress. That's not to say you shouldn't pay attention to slipups and evolve from them; just that you shouldn't define yourself by them when they happen. Whether you just unwittingly offended a colleague or got fired, the long-view approach is the same: acknowledge the unfortunate setback and remedy what you can.

FIELD-TEST TAKING THE LONG VIEW HERE:

Write about a setback, and then write a possible long-view perspective. (Possible long views: "Not going to spinning class today is just one missed workout." "I am more complex than one piece of negative feedback.")

____

____

____

Write about another setback along with a long-view reframe here:

____

____

____

[7] *Muhammad Ali*, directed by Ken Burns, Sarah Bruns, and David McMahon, PBS, (2021; Florentine Films and WETA), https://www.pbs.org/kenburns/muhammad-ali/.

Attorney in Action

Corporate attorney Dana received the worst performance review of her career from an onerous new boss. Known for her impeccable reputation, she was convinced initially that a departure from her excellent record would scar her forever. When Dana realized that one undesirable performance review did not have to define her, she stopped panicking and became accepting of the unavoidable speed bumps on a committed career path. Then she was able to center on changing her behavior according to her boss's appraisal. She finds that she is easier on herself now, which helps her to excel more creatively and with less pressure.

LAWYER LIKE AN ATHLETE THOUGHT-CONDITIONING PRINCIPLE #6

Lock It In

There's so much riding on every competition for a professional athlete that they need to be fully present at game time, ready to instantly swat away any kind of thought that might distract them from their objective, or they can lose out. There is no time when an athlete is in the heat of the actual game to be reflective; it's about being completely reflexive. Gold medal skier Lindsey Vonn conveys the importance of not letting thoughts steal crucial time by advising, "When you fall, get right back up. Just keep going, keep pushing it."[8]

A classic tennis trick is counting racket strings to divert from possible self-defeating thoughts between points; and some golfers are known to strike up casual conversations to drown out anticipatory nervousness before tournaments start. One of the most effective ways that athletes put self-defeating thoughts right back on a positive track when every second counts is by repeating a favorite mantra—"It's okay. Stay steady. Keep the pace. It's behind me now."—to snap immediately back into a winning current. Such strategies are just as crucial for rubber-hitting-the-road attorney work requiring absolute focus on what needs to be done right here,

---

[8] "Lindsey Vonn on Ski Racing and Why We Love the Sport," *Arctica*, October 12, 2014, https://arctica.com/blog/lindsey-vonns-inspiring-words-on-ski-racing-remind-us-why-we-love-the-sport/.

right now. When you need to be present for an acutely vulnerable client or you're speaking in court with no chance for a redo, you have no room for any thoughts that might pull your attention away. Your emphasis, when the pressure is absolute, must be entirely on what you are doing, motion by motion, so that you are fully prepared to channel each moment into ramping up.

FIELD-TEST MAKING IT ABOUT THE MOMENT HERE:

List a mantra or two that you can use to recalibrate being back to the moment instead of getting sidetracked. (For example, "I'm getting there." "I am getting through this." "One thing at a time.")

____

____

____

List ways you can divert yourself from unhelpful thoughts while you're waiting to engage in an important next work step. (For example, counting ceiling tiles or something else in the room; playing your favorite song in your head)

____

____

____

Write your own ways of diverting yourself:

____

____

____

What thought conditioning essentially comes down to, I tell my client Sarah, the maxed-out immigration attorney you met at the start of this chapter, is preparing your brain, every attorney's most precious asset, for exceptional performance. When you practice the principles we've covered here, resolutely and with priority, you will find yourself thinking evermore clearly, sharply, and innovatively. It's worth saying one more time

Attorney in Action

Sabrina, an independent investigator on sexual misconduct cases, found it triggering to interview victims of sexual assault. As a victim of sexual assault herself, she struggled with staying on task and not letting her feelings compromise her concentration. Sabrina discovered that saying a mantra to herself—"Ask and listen, ask and listen"—kept her anchored in an objective space during even the most heart-wrenching interviews. Because she was now less disrupted internally, she could be more present in interviews and more accurate with her reports.

that thought conditioning is not a quick fix, and valuing the concepts and vowing to apply them is not enough. You've got to stay right on top of your thoughts, nipping those destructive ones in the bud before they can obstruct you, to curate a mental climate that will bring out your best.

Though you will always be susceptible to self-defeating talk, and the countless disruptions of law and our busy culture, your proficiency with dismissing irrelevant inner clamor will evolve with diligent rehearsal. Naomi Osaka, entrenched in serious thought conditioning her entire esteemed career, says she still needs to learn "how to deal with not being 100 percent" by training her brain to serve her better than criticism, doubt, regret, and fear when she falters.[9] Just like Osaka and every other noteworthy athlete, you too will need to keep at it if you want to come out on top and triumph.

Good news: we've officially covered the essentials of thinking in ways that lighten your load and maximize your success. As always, please take a breather so that you can begin to absorb all this new information. When you feel sufficiently ready to take in more, the next chapter will show you how to reinforce the mindset you're working on by adapting your surroundings.

---

[9] *Naomi Osaka*, directed by Garrett Bradley (Netflix Series, 2021), https://www.netflix.com/title/81128594.

7

Cultivate Winning Ecosystems

As our world becomes increasingly hybrid, whatever lines that once existed between work and home are hopelessly blurred, which makes having our personal and professional lives equally weighted like a yin-yang symbol unrealistic. Maybe when we literally worked in cities and lived in suburbs, way before technology made us accessible from anywhere around the clock, we may have achieved some semblance of that kind of compartmentalization. But now, with less and less in our culture supporting such an even-keeled existence, striving to separate work from home completely only leads to exhaustion and disappointment. Work and life are now impossibly intertwined, and there's really no healthy way to push them apart.

While pursuing that old-fashioned kind of balance is a fool's errand that merely froths up already existing stress, there is a new and better brand of equilibrium that is actually much more satisfying and possible to achieve. Close your eyes for a moment, and notice the feelings that arise when you reflect on the very concept of balance, and you will quickly see that it's an inner state you're after, which, as you've learned by now, is completely under your purview. Alter the way you think about balance, as an interior experience over which you have say, and you have a new kind of superpower to feel grounded in a pleasing

> “Alter the way you think about balance, as an interior experience over which you have say, and you have a new kind of superpower.”

work/life symmetry—even in a culture that discourages balance at every turn.

If you want to feel composed amid the constant disruptions of being a lawyer, you can take charge by asking these central questions:

- *What can you alter in your surrounding environments to bring about the feelings and thoughts you want to have?*
- *How can you construct the structures around you to energize, propel, and inspire you?*
- *How can you create contexts in which you are most likely to thrive?*
- *What sort of atmospheres will be conducive to you being at your best?*

There are plenty of sports champions who can afford a lot of luxury, but it's not necessarily expensive trappings that bring them inner balance. Major League baseball pitcher Andrew Chafin prefers to live in an RV in the woods rather than a mansion because he loves the silence and simplicity of the forest.[1] Olympic snowboarder Lindsey Jacobellis hangs out in her backyard and is invigorated by a gurgling fountain.[2] Whatever it takes to make your main habitats sources of interior harmony is an individual choice—entirely up to you and not necessarily dictated by how much money you have in the bank.

The way to start is by clearing the decks of what's not working so you can free up space for what does work. This means defining what in your surrounding environments is compromising you even a little—whether it's an uncomfortable chair, a paint color you've grown tired of, or a sticky note that should have been pulled off months ago—and get rid of it. The upshot is anything that doesn't serve an essential purpose and/or stimulate you to lawyer like an athlete must go. As we've established, anything unnecessarily taking up your time and attention is only getting in your way, as you realize the work of this book by really digging in and doing things differently.

---

[1] Cody Stavenhagen, "Tigers Pitcher Andrew Chafin Is Eccentric, Authentic and Very Good At His Job," *The Athletic*, June 1, 2022, https://theathletic.com/3342765/2022/06/01/tigers-andrew-chafin-mlb/.

[2] Sarah Sekula, "How Six Top Athletes Relax and Recover," *ESPN.com*, April 19, 2017, https://www.espn.com/espnw/life-style/story/_/id/19193888/how-six-top-athletes-relax-recover.

To get a grasp on what is essential if you are to be a steadier and more collected version of you, grab your pen and a timer. For each prompt below, set your timer for two minutes, and write without stopping until the timer goes off.

Here is your first prompt:

What must you absolutely have in your life to feel more internally balanced?

When your two minutes are up, set the timer for two minutes again, and go with this prompt:

What must you absolutely remove from your life to feel more internally balanced?

Once you've completed this short exercise, you can apply the tiny-step method to anything on your list—choosing one little alteration at a time—and start seeing results from your curating.

What is one thing around you that you can discard right now to feel better? (examples: fast-food trash in your car, an outdated photo in a frame on your desk, dessert in your fridge you don't want tempting you)

____

____

____

What is something you can bring into your surroundings right now to feel better? (examples: music that takes you back to happy memories, drawer dividers for more order, natural light and fresh air)

____

____

____

You can further implore the thoughts and feelings you want by assessing the settings where you spend most of your time. How well are those settings serving you?

Whatever you identify that is draining you, even ever so slightly, you must regard it as an unwieldy weed in your garden and pull it out lest it pull you off course even a little bit. Then think of what you want to plant in your life to accomplish your goals more easily.

Here are some suggestions to get you going:

Enliven your senses. Approach the environments you spend the most time in with the intent to improve your sensory experience. Former San Diego Charger Nick Hardwick immerses himself more fully in at-home yoga sessions by cranking his favorite musician on his sound system.[3] Maybe you put fresh flowers on your desk, cook with exotic spices, or listen to a "creativity" playlist while you're typing a brief. Any small way you can delight your ears, nose, and eyes will lift your thoughts and mood.

[3] Jamie Gold, "Elite Athletes At Home," *San Diego Union-Tribune*, February 21, 2019, https://www.sandiegouniontribune.com/lifestyle/home-and-garden/sd-hm-athletes-home-20190221-story.html.

Spark a refreshing outlook. Adorn the environments you spend the most time in to stimulate your imagination. Serena Williams's home is graced with evocative modern art.[4] You might hang art or photos that recall whimsy and wonder; put books, movies, and podcasts within reach that stir your mind and heart; bring in furniture that lets you sink in and escape daily worries.

Tailor with precision. As you're considering environmental changes you may want to make, start with the particular inner experience you're after. Many athletes have dedicated at-home gyms professionally appointed to put them in workout mode.[5] If respite after a long day is your goal, on the other hand, you'll want to make sure every aspect of your living room winds you down. If the goal is efficiency and focus on the job, you will want to create a workspace that keeps you awake and alert.

Be practical. While you're modifying your surroundings in the ways I'm suggesting, it's important to consider mundane but essential details to keep you healthy. Ironman world champ Michellie Jones has hardwood floors throughout her house because she is asthmatic and can't be exposed to allergens found in carpeting.[6] For you, if you're working from home, your first step is to build privacy into the equation by having your office in a room that serves no other purpose and has a door that locks. If the main reason you're stressed in your car is that you've been putting off a mounting mechanical problem that could blow any day, you'll want to take your car to a garage for fixing. When you treat the environments you frequent with care, they treat you well in return.

Appreciate your agency. Rather than feeling discouraged because there's not much you can do to improve your surroundings if you work in a cubicle or live with a slob, trust there are still ways you

---

[4] Jay Wilson, "Pro Athletes With Awe-Inspiring Homes," *House Digest*, August 26, 2021, https://www.housedigest.com/586586/pro-athletes-with-awe-inspiring-homes/.

[5] Amanda Lybeck, "Pro Athlete Homes: From Amazing Fitness Rooms And Outdoor Sports Courts To Unique Luxury Branding," Realogics SIR, February 26, 2016, https://www.rsir.com/blog/pro-athlete-homes-from-amazing-fitness-rooms-and-outdoor-sports-courts-to-unique-luxury-branding/.

[6] Jamie Gold, "Elite Athletes At Home," *San Diego Union-Tribune*, February 21, 2019, https://www.sandiegouniontribune.com/lifestyle/home-and-garden/sd-hm-athletes-home-20190221-story.html.

can have some say. Athletes maximize their autonomy on commercial flights by wearing their most comfy clothes, setting their own entertainment up on their laptops, and bringing their own nutritious snacks.[7] You can assert yourself similarly by, let's say, adding your own personal touches wherever you can or keeping your desk surface clean. Even when you don't have full free reign over your environment, tiny tweaks can still engage and uplift you.

Now, let's get an overview of what some overall refinement to the environments in which you spend the most time might look like. I want you to think big picture here, so just go with your impulses, and don't be concerned with time, budget, or other pragmatics. Once you've completed your brainstorming, we'll zero in on what's simultaneously possible and appealing right now.

We'll do this by playing what I call the circle game.

You'll need that timer again for this one, and then proceed:

The headings atop three upcoming pages are the settings I'm presuming you function in most often: home, workspace, car. For each of these three settings, you'll write on the inside of the circle below the heading what you want to be thinking and feeling in that specific area. On the outside of the circle, you'll write down what outer factors—décor, equipment, accents, ambiance—will promote that internal state.

Here are examples of what might come to mind for the inside of your home circle when you consider the overall internal experience you want to have at home: unhurried, uplifted, at ease. Next, here's what you might land on for the inside of your workspace circle when you imagine the inner landscape you want to have in your workspace: excited, purposeful, ready to go. Perhaps for the inside of your car circle, you ponder the internal state you desire while you're driving: awake, alert, able to let my thoughts be.

Once you've filled the inside of your home, work, and car circles with the elements that make up the internal states you want to experience in each of those spaces, you'll need to figure out what factors in those environments will help you achieve your preferred inner states. If you want your home to feel more like a retreat, you might decide on reducing clutter and purchasing some luxurious bedding. Feeling more motivated while you're working might amount to bringing in a kick-ass headset for online

---

[7] Natalie B. Compton, "How to Travel in Style Like a Pro Athlete," *GQ*, November 28. 2017, https://www.gq.com/story/travel-advice-pro-athletes.

meetings along with your favorite coffee mug. And to encourage better thoughts and feelings in your car? Smart attorneys (and athletes too) begin by keeping off the air anything that might agitate them, and using that valuable windshield time instead to loosen up, abiding by a strict no-news policy so they don't have to think about hot-button issues. Whatever those surrounding components happen to be for you, you'll write them around your home, workspace, and car circles.

You're the architect of your own life here, setting out to refashion and renovate your surroundings to more your liking. This is all about you and what you really know deep down you need and want to be happy and productive. You may have to negotiate with those whom you live, work, and travel to make some of the ecosystem changes you want, and that's not always easy. It's important, though, that for now you just let yourself go with this, and rest assured we will get to the other people part later.

Borrowing from the work-plus spirit, play the circle game in a manner most likely to let you be still and coax out your most intuitive and therefore well-advised ideas. Perhaps that kind of situation involves putting on clothes that signify play more than work, sitting at a table with a window view, or going to a place you don't frequent so that you can get some distance. Only you know what will serve and sustain you; turn the page when you're ready to map out the winning ecosystems for your primary places.

Before you begin, just to ensure you've got the rules down, I'll share circles completed by some of my attorney coaching clients. We'll start with the car ecosystem since that is usually the easiest:

Attorney in Action

New associate Paige loved the experience she was getting at a firm in the center of Atlanta, but her commute through awful traffic was wearing her down. She wanted coaching to ease her nerves so that she could feel steadier at work. We discussed what she could do to make her commute less nail-biting, and she decided to try taking a little longer but less congested route. Having her car detailed helped her to feel more comfortable in her car, and she discovered that alternating between listening to amusing podcasts and just enjoying silence made her travel time a nicer way to segue between home and work.

Attorney in Action (Cont'd)

Paige's Winning Car Ecosystem

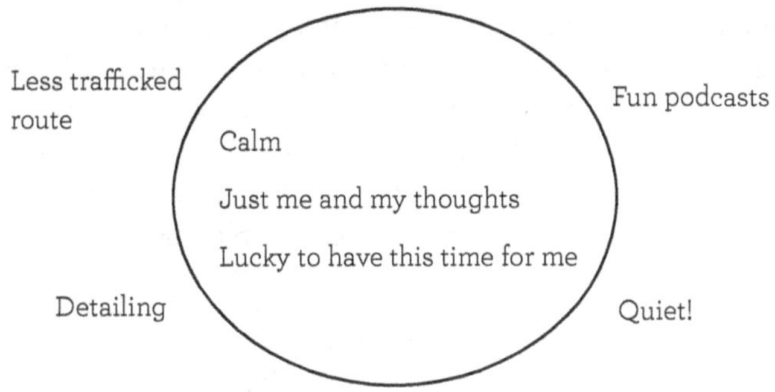

Your Winning Car Ecosystem

Now that you've seen Paige's winning car ecosystem, design your winning car ecosystem here:

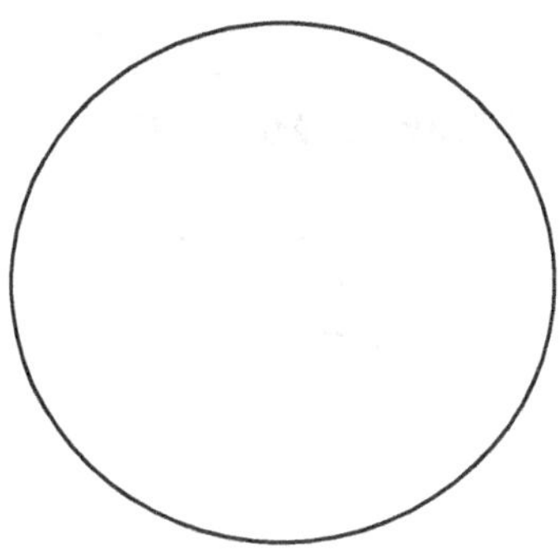

Write inside the circle: Thoughts and feelings you want to have in your car.

Write outside the circle: External factors that will encourage the thoughts and feelings you want to have in your car.

Attorney in Action

Solo practitioner Holly sought my coaching help to ride the waves of early entrepreneurship more smoothly. I asked her what she might do to make her apartment a safer harbor, and she recalled that she'd loved the soothing aroma of pine trees surrounding her childhood home. She was surprised to learn that lighting a pine-scented candle at home in the evening helped her to calm down. From a more relaxed state of mind, she identified other ways to make her house a respite from uncertainty: putting a couple of throws in her drafty living room, reading soothing books before bed, and replacing an unreliable blender.

Holly's Winning Home Ecosystem

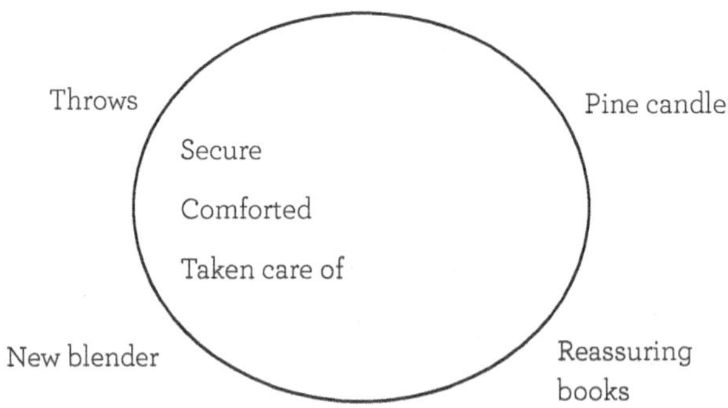

Your Winning Home Ecosystem

Now that you've seen Holly's winning home circle, design your winning home circle here:

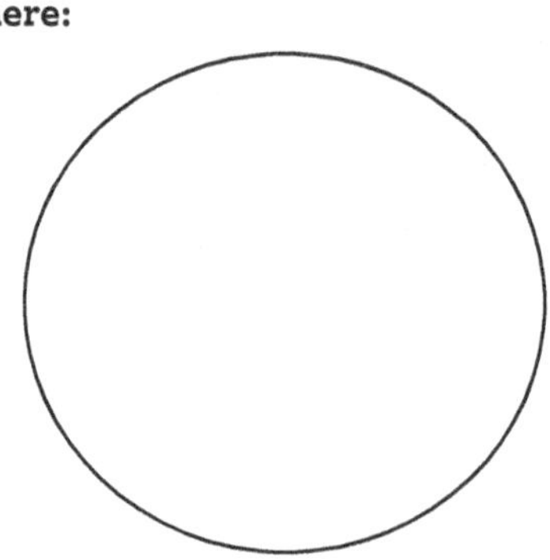

Write inside the circle: Thoughts and feelings you want to have at home.

Write outside the circle: External factors that will encourage the thoughts and feelings you want to have at home.

When you're confident you've taken the time you need, you will probably end up with a crowded list of internals and externals. Your next step is to start turning your externals into actionable tiny-step environmental upgrades.

List three external tiny steps you can take to achieve the internal state you want:

In your car:

1. ______________________________
2. ______________________________
3. ______________________________

Attorney in Action

Ramsey, an in-house attorney for a rapidly growing healthcare organization, needed coaching to stay on task in a workplace situation where he didn't have much privacy. With his office "in the middle of everything" and people coming at him from every department with problems, his challenge was getting into an ultra-attentive work mode despite those distractions. He discovered that by keeping his door closed more often, hanging a painting of a pristine outdoor scene, and putting some files away, he could feel more composed in his office. Turning off the jarring fluorescent lights above him and opting for lamps also helped, as did eventually getting a friendlier desk chair. The more he made his office his own, the greater the sense of command and ease he enjoyed there, and the better his output.

Ramsey's Winning Workspace Ecosystem

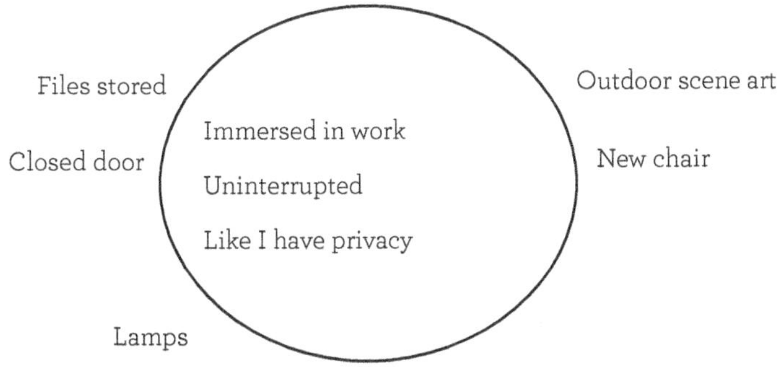

Attorney in Action (Cont'd)

Your Winning Workspace Ecosystem

Now that you've seen Ramsey's winning workspace ecosystem, design your winning workspace ecosystem here:

Write inside the circle: Thoughts and feelings you want to have at work.

Write outside the circle: External factors that will encourage the thoughts and feelings you want to have at work.

Once you've completed your car, home, and workspace circles, give yourself a few days to let additional insights emerge. When you create the right conditions to gently shake up your mind like a snow globe, it's wise to allow still-forming ideas to settle and land.

At home:

1. ______________________________
2. ______________________________
3. ______________________________

In your workspace:

1. ______________________________
2. ______________________________
3. ______________________________

> "The advantage of living in a world of overwhelming options is that you can curate from the outside only what you know aligns with goals for your inside."

As you execute your tiny steps, you will see that the more you nurture your inner world in ways that feel fortifying, the more likely you are to encounter the equilibrium you seek. The advantage of living in a world of overwhelming options is that you can curate from the outside only what you know aligns with goals for your inside.

If you consistently tend to those domains you function in most, replacing the redundant with the relevant, clearing out what smacks of cacophony, that appealing sense of balance we all want will no longer be elusive. As we've covered, it's not possible, whether you're an attorney or not, to feel perpetually poised or on top of everything all the time, but there's a load of distress you can diminish by readying your brain and psyche for equanimity.

You will get a gratifying taste of balance from spending some serious, unhurried time with this chapter. Keep looking at those home, work, and car circles you drew up, standing back and considering, crossing out and adding and testing them out, and you will find yourself moving evermore easily in sync with your blueprints. By asserting command over your surroundings, you will learn one more vital way to trade stress for sustenance.

With your winning ecosystems in place, the next chapter asks you to move beyond making cosmetic changes in those environments you function in most. We'll dig into another critical aspect of your life and work that impacts how you think and feel: your interactions and relationships with those around you.

8

Recruit a Robust Team

Inevitably when attorneys come to me for coaching, no matter what the issue, from "I want to feel more poised when speaking in front of a group" to "I am at the burnout wall and have no idea what to do," it often comes down to a factor that can't ever really be controlled: other human beings. Everything you've applied from this book up to this chapter has been improving your work and life in ways that *are* entirely within your control:

- Getting less ensnared by time-wasting activities
- Making better decisions concerning how you treat yourself
- Ridding yourself of needless distractions
- Stepping outside your immediate thoughts to see and act on broader perspectives
- Doing what you can with what you're in charge of to feel and be more successful

By now, if you're really mobilizing this book and seeing results, you are starting to get along better with yourself. From a more self-assured place, you are probably seeing that people generally fall into two groups: those who ease you forward and those who hold you back. It's time to apply your more grounded and discerning self to assessing your social world and seeing where you can reduce friction and maximize the good.

If you have the same mindset as many of my attorney clients who regard social time as trivial, you may need some convincing. So let me present my case for making thriving relationships part of the work-plus model.

Every psychology student learns that early attachment is the biggest predictor of success. Anything less than feeling taken care of by your primary caretakers in infancy and you will have some difficulty believing in yourself and others. Without the assuredness and self-possession that comes from knowing you are safe and supported no matter what, you may be wary of others out in the world. This is a problem since people are everywhere, and we are all built to be social animals. Whether we like it or not, we must regularly associate with human beings to feel okay, get things done, and experience a sense of belonging and meaning.

Professional athletes certainly know that harmonious interpersonal relationships are directly related to their achievement. We observe the full-on importance of human connection for athletes quite literally when a team of cooperating members accomplishes much more than individual members could have done on their own. We also see that even the most talented athletes can't lead their team to the top when a winning mix of team skills and camaraderie isn't in place. Of course, we notice the entourages comprised of all sorts of coaches and specialists, family members and friends that encircle every professional athlete. (As a 2014 study of Olympians shows, the entourage supports the athlete in doing their best and is one of the most crucial components of sports success.[1])

What always stands out to me when I watch sports documentaries is how well those entourages are distilled down to a tight group of people unified in the same direction. Sophia Jowett, professor of psychology at Loughborough University, cites research showing that "healthy relationships among coaches and athletes, parents and athletes, partners and athletes are nurturing, supporting, rewarding, comforting, motivating, and fulfilling. Such social and personal relationships are all linked with low levels of depression and stress and high levels of vitality and satisfaction, a vital part of health and wellbeing."[2]

We all know from the media just how disruptive problem relationships can be to a professional athlete's career, whether with a fed-up spouse,

---

[1] Caroline Weppner, "Who's Got My Back? Part 3: Friends & Family," Mpowher Athlete, n.d., https://www.mpowherathlete.com/mpowher-blog/athlete-friends-family-relationship.

[2] Sophia Jowett, "Relationships in Sport and Exercise: Their Value and Significance to Health and Wellbeing," LinkedIn, January 1, 2016, https://www.linkedin.com/pulse/relationships-sport-exercise-value-significance-health-sophia-jowett/.

an incompetent coach, or a crooked accountant. The most successful athletes make sure to surround themselves with positive and supportive people, and they treat those people very well. When issues emerge in those relationships, star sports figures confront them immediately so they don't become an obstruction.

"You wouldn't argue with me if I were to say that no athlete could rise to the top in isolation, so trust me on this one: every attorney needs an entourage too."

You wouldn't argue with me if I were to say that no athlete could rise to the top in isolation, so trust me on this one: every attorney needs an entourage too.

You can't lawyer like an athlete alone. Nor can you lawyer like an athlete without conscientiously ensuring that the prominent people in your life are giving you pleasure and purpose rather than problems and pain. People are complicated and unpredictable, and that includes you, so there is no perfection here.

By following the strategies below, beginning with the clearing out as we always do, you can build your own entourage to smooth your way ahead:

Identify the obvious obstructors: Is there anyone in your life or at work who asks too much of you or is a drag to be around? Unless you absolutely must interact with these people (e.g., a micromanaging boss, a know-it-all relative at family functions, a gossipy neighbor), you have to find a way to remove them from your orbit because they're causing you undue stress. It's harder if you feel obligated to the people making things harder for you, but you really can't afford to give your limited time and attention to those who to any degree pull you off your path.

Set boundaries: Curtailing or cutting out exposure to detrimental people doesn't mean that you have to be insensitive or start ghosting everyone. It's simply a matter of continuing with the question this book keeps asking: *how can you rearrange things to get better outcomes?* With people, that's a matter of designing your relationships with others to suit you. How often do you want to see the people in your life; what do you want to do when you're with them? Even for those people you wish to reduce time with but can't, you can still regulate to some extent how they treat you. It may help to point out here that setting boundaries amounts to being assertive, though it's often misunderstood as aggression.

For the record, assertiveness is the art of setting limits for yourself that are respectful to you and others. Aggression is making disrespectful demands, crossing someone else's boundaries in a pushy manner. Assertiveness at its most basic is saying, "I'd appreciate it if you could text me a heads-up next time you're running late" or "I'd prefer we don't meet at a bar because I don't want to drink." At a more complex level, assertiveness is saying anything from "Unfortunately, I won't be able to stay at the family reunion all day this year, but I can swing by for a couple of hours" to "If you reach a point where you can converse with me without raising your voice, I am up for continuing our discussion."

Expect resistance to your boundaries at first: Quite often when you exercise your assertiveness by setting healthy limits, interactions and relationships get better because others are inspired to similarly respect themselves and you. However, there are always people who, in response to your elevated expectations, may not like that you are changing up the dynamics—especially if they have been getting away with bad behavior they don't want to admit to or stop. The way to look at it is that some people will become more unified in your direction as you clarify your parameters, and the less aligned will drop off. Boundaries can cause turbulence when long-standing patterns are interrupted, but the more you assert your limits, the more your social world adjusts to support you.

"Boundaries can cause turbulence when long-standing patterns are interrupted, but the more you assert your limits, the more your social world adjusts to support you."

Now that you have a better idea of what it means to protect yourself by drawing lines in the sand, let's get a clearer view of where you might want to start implementing boundaries with the people in your life:

Who do you currently spend the most time with at work?

____

____

____

Attorney in Action

Affable attorney Henry initiated coaching with me to address habits that were compromising his work performance. Once he accomplished individual improvements like eating better and exercising more, he realized that a necessary and more challenging change would be to stop being overly accommodating to colleagues. He was known at his firm for picking up the slack, pitching in, and stepping in to work on a weekend when someone else wanted to take the day off. It was great to feel appreciated all the time but at what cost? By being too available and agreeable, Henry was chronically prioritizing his coworkers over himself, and it had to stop. When Henry started scaling back his availability to a reasonable team-player level, some colleagues got testy with him, accusing him of not being helpful or reliable anymore. I advised him to persist with his healthier boundaries, pointing out that it takes time for people to adapt and that Henry couldn't afford to cave. Fortunately, most people at work responded considerately to Henry, admiring him for no longer allowing himself to be taken advantage of. Through standing his ground at work, no matter how much he was tempted to go back to being a pushover, Henry grew steadily more confident and was able to approach his own work with greater commitment.

Out of all those people, with whom do you least enjoy interacting?

____

____

____

How can you limit time with these people?

____

____

____

Who do you spend the most time with in your personal life?

____

____

____

Out of all those people, with whom do you least enjoy interacting?

____

____

____

How can you limit time with those people?

____

____

____

With boundaries that minimize contact with people not aligned with you, you will have more time for the people you *do* want in your life.

Here are strategies for making those relationships—at work, home, in the community, wherever you happen to be—more mutually rewarding. The skills herein will also serve you well when navigating those trying people with whom you must interact:

Recognize that we're all after the same thing: Always keep in mind why secure bonding during infancy is so foundational. All of us want and need to feel connected, part of something bigger than ourselves, safe enough to venture forth and try new things, in the company of people who truly care for us and are there for us. When you approach all of your relationships with a desire to create that experience for others by being genuine, reliable, trustworthy, and giving (without compromising yourself too much), everybody wins. There is no hard-and-fast rule for reciprocation in a relationship; there is no 50/50 quid pro quo, and the give-and-take of any relationship is greater than the sum of its parts, with both parties accountable. A good general rule for relationship satisfaction is you should never expect another person to complete you; the best relationships are icing on the cake of a solid relationship with yourself.

"All of us want and need to feel connected, part of something bigger than ourselves, safe enough to venture forth and try new things, in the company of people who truly care for us and are there for us."

Accept responsibility: Most of the time when relationships come up in coaching, the angle is that other people are creating problems, and everything would be easier if they would just stop misbehaving. While it's true that there are those out there who make our lives harder, our displeasure in social situations is not always the fault of others. You might say, what about the mean boss or the cheating partner? My response is that such bad behavior is, at the very least, enabled by the people who put up with it.

The healthiest of personalities are those that can bend and flex without losing their integrity in response to the inevitable trials of work and life. The unhealthiest personalities are those that can't bend and flex without becoming overly rigid or breaking altogether. Someone with a functional personality is able to acknowledge when inner growth and change are necessary to improve a situation and then act on that. Someone with a dysfunctional personality may recognize the need to evolve but doesn't want to do the inner work, and so blames others for problems they are unequipped or unwilling to own.

We've gone over the importance in past chapters of looking at feedback or criticism head-on, considering it carefully, and taking in the relevant information to reflect on and resolve, rather than tossing it all out defensively. Well, this skill is especially critical in relationships where you must accept your responsibility for a thorny dynamic. The more you are accountable for your part and set boundaries that allow others to handle their part, the healthier your relationships will be.

Listen mindfully: It is human nature when you are talking to others to want to give your opinion, share your thoughts, and be heard and validated. That tendency to want attention and approval is amplified when someone is angry or accusatory and you want to jump in and save face. The tendency is *even* stronger when someone is upset and hurting, and you want to resolve the problem to relieve their pain. The thing here is that listening is more beneficial to others than leaping in

"The more you are accountable for your part and set boundaries that allow others to handle their part, the healthier your relationships will be."

and trying to convince or fix. Listening allows people to express themselves, and it allows you to understand what a person is saying before you respond.

Empathize: Listening starts the process of understanding someone, but empathy takes listening to the next step of trying to identify with the other person's lived experience. Have you ever summed up someone from a distance, deciding, for example, that because a person on social media opposes your convictions, you don't want anything more to do with them? Have you ever made a negative judgment about someone only to realize later that you didn't have certain facts that would have led you to a more positive appraisal?

Often misconstrued as sympathy, empathy doesn't mean that you feel sorry for, agree with, or even like someone. Empathy is about taking the time, asking questions, and letting the answers sink in to understand someone so that you can relate to them in a more accurate, nuanced way. Real empathy is being able to say to someone, "I've never been through what you're going through, but I know from my own struggles how hard it can be to feel hopeful during tough times" or "Thank you for taking the time to explain why you voted that way. It helps to know where you're coming from." So powerful is empathy that athletic coaches are best able to build trust and stimulate performance by simply listening when players need to process and vent.[3]

Express appreciation: There's an accepted simple formula among marital therapists that the most resilient marriages are those where gratitude is expressed more than complaints. We've established that human beings have to work hard at reaping the benefits of positivity, but it pays off especially well when it comes to relationships. A beautiful example of this kind of thinking can be found in the words of Usain Bolt, considered to be the greatest sprinter of all time, who said, "To all my doubters, thank you very

---

[3] Jason Kelly, "Coaches Use the Power of Empathy to Inspire," Stack, June 11, 2021, https://www.stack.com/a/coaches-use-the-power-of-empathy-to-inspire/.

much because you guys have also pushed me."[4] We can find incentive even when people are skeptical.

Get comfortable with conflict: Disagreements are a natural part of relationships because all of us, no matter how much we have in common, are different. When people who respect each other communicate their differences, innovative solutions and better ways of getting along can emerge. It can be arduous to do conflict smoothly, particularly when emotions are running high. Constructive conflict comes down to bringing issues up as they arise and talking about them in a civilized manner, sometimes over several conversations to allow for cooling down if needed, as you arrive at acceptable compromises.

Next, to get an idea of how you can apply these strategies to improve your existing relationships, consider these questions:

Is there an issue that keeps coming up in your relationships that signals something you might need to change about yourself?

____

____

____

How do you push the buttons of other people?

____

____

____

What do your closest allies say you need to work on in yourself to have more successful relationships?

____

____

____

[4] "Sports Quotes for Thank You," QuotesGram, n.d., https://quotesgram.com/img/sports-quotes-for-thank-you/5624931/.

Are there boundaries set by others that you could take more seriously to improve your relationships?

____

____

____

How can you be more present in your relationships?

____

____

____

Think of a relationship where you could stand to expand your view of another's circumstances. What questions might you ask to get that greater understanding?

____

____

____

____

How can you show greater empathy in your relationships?

____

____

____

Have you been avoiding conflict in any of your relationships? If so, how can you address that conflict constructively?

____

____

____

What can you do to show appreciation for an important person in your personal life?

____

____

____

Attorney in Action

Madelyn, a married personal injury attorney with three children, found that the more she tried to apply what she was learning from me through coaching, the more fraught her marriage was becoming with arguments. Her partner felt that he was picking up too much slack with taking care of the kids as Madelyn increasingly worked on developing healthier habits for herself. She was beginning to wonder if coaching was really a good idea when it was causing friction in her marriage that hadn't been there before. Madelyn realized through our discussions that she needed to work with her partner to arrive at new ways of handling domestic responsibilities that simultaneously allowed her to continue on her personal and professional improvement path and were fair and equitable for him. Through a series of conversations where Madelyn and her partner took turns sharing their perspectives, they negotiated new ground rules that both of them could happily live with. This saved time in the long run because addressing the conflict helped them to coexist more harmoniously.

What can you do to show appreciation for an important relationship in your professional life?

____

____

____

Now that you have some ideas for enhancing your personal and professional relationships, let's look at this entourage you're upgrading with respect to how you might round it out with necessary assistance. Do you need healthcare specialists beyond your primary care physician and dentist? Do you need help with yard work, snow removal, cooking, or childcare? Is it time to break up with your hair stylist or financial advisor and find more capable replacements? Remember, you can't do it all alone, and you are most apt to succeed when you surround yourself with the right people. Just like with every successful athlete, family, friends, and colleagues in your corner are not enough. You may also need qualified hired help to achieve your goals.

Attorney in Action

Mei, a public defender not making nearly the salary she had hoped, balked when I suggested at one of our coaching sessions that she hire someone to clean her house. She argued that regular coaching was already a stretch for her, and it wouldn't be practical to pay a cleaning person when she was perfectly capable of cleaning her house herself. She realized the wisdom, though, of paying for a service that would allow her more time to rack up billable hours—at an hourly rate much higher than what she would pay the cleaning person. She gave it a try, and it didn't take her long to see the value of her investment. Not only did Mei have more work time, but she was less stressed by the pressure to keep her house looking presentable.

"The more you are in the company of people you can be yourself with, the freer and more encouraged you will feel to move toward what you want."

Relationships are so integral to happiness and productivity that this chapter can't say all there is to say on the subject. So, as we wrap up here, I will sum up four bottom lines to always work from:

First, for peak performance and fulfillment in your life and work, pinpoint all the people you know who allow you to just be you without having to be "on." The more you are in the company of people you can be yourself with, the freer and more encouraged you will feel to move toward what you want. Beyond the equilibrium of your favorite people having your back, regularly letting your guard down allows space for curiosity, creativity, imagination, and intuition—all of which improve your work.

Second, no matter how well you get along with yourself and other people, there will be some relationship problems you will never be able to solve. You can't force yourself to feel relationship chemistry if it's not there. You can't be content in a relationship where another person is unwilling or unable to see you as you want to be seen. Most important here, there is nothing you can do, no intervention or ultimatum, no personal change you can make to turn around an abuser.

I mentioned earlier that people with functional personalities are self-aware and responsible in relationships, whereas people with dysfunctional personalities are less in touch with themselves and prone to put responsibility on others. An abuser is someone who through guilt, manipulation, insult, and other types of harm makes others feel that whatever is going wrong is always their fault.

The physical abuser will say you deserved it, drove them to it, or it was just their passion for you gone awry, and it will never happen again. The gaslighter will make you question your sanity by accusing you of misunderstanding, taking things too seriously, or overreacting when you have levelheaded doubts, impulses, and requests. Physical abuse is easy to identify because it's right there in black and white. Emotional abuse can be hard to pin down because it's so subtle and insidious.

Typically, you know you're in an abusive relationship if you feel chronically demeaned, tricked, confused, like you're walking on eggshells, and unsure of yourself. If you think you may be in an abusive relationship, call the National Domestic Violence Hotline at 800-799-7233. They are experts at assessing for abuse and will tell you what you're up against and what to do. Most of the time with abusers, whether you're in an abusive intimate, platonic, or work relationship, it's wise to consult with a therapist to come up with an exit plan.

Lastly, there is a loneliness epidemic going on in our culture right now from less reliable social institutions and increasing technology—all of which was exacerbated during the COVID-19 pandemic. We were on our way to a hybrid world anyway, but quarantine brought this new frontier about much sooner than expected. The result is it's not as easy as it once was to be out there getting the contact we need with each other, and so you have to regard that contact as a necessary vitamin you can't live without. Taking that vitamin means deliberately planning to be with other people—at home, at work, at concerts and sporting events, or simply walking down sidewalks together. Add

> "It's not as easy as it once was to be out in the world getting the contact we need with each other, and so you have to regard that contact as a necessary vitamin you can't live without and make it happen."

to the hybrid nature of life these days that you are busier than most people with work, and it's not just going to happen unless you make it happen. As Ironman coach Andrejs Birjukovs emphasizes, "You must create time for people, schedule everything in."[5]

Like all components of the work-plus model, having thriving relationships is a permanent undertaking that is never done. However, the more you put into that undertaking, the more you will see evidence that the caliber of your relationships is directly proportional to the caliber of your life and work. In the next chapter, we'll take this emphasis further by identifying the assets you see in yourself and others, and galvanizing and combining those assets for even better results.

[5] Andrejs Birjukovs, "18 Practical Time Management Hacks for Athletes and Busy People,"; The Athlete Blog, n.d., https://theathleteblog.com/time-management-hacks-for-athletes/.

9

Lead with Your Strengths

Ken Dryden is a hockey Hall-of-Famer celebrated for his uncommon feats as a goalie, arguably the most critical position on the ice. Unparalleled at his capacity to stop the puck, he led the Montreal Canadiens to six Stanley Cups and won the Vezina Trophy (at the time, awarded to the goalie who allowed the fewest goals) five times. Like all elite athletes, Dryden excelled because he figured out early on what he was best at in his sport. He then determined what came most naturally to him in hockey and perfected the particulars of that skill: positioning, moving laterally, covering angles, following and anticipating the action in front of him, and preventing the opposition from scoring. (If that goalie job description sounds familiar, consider that Dryden became an attorney after his hockey career and excelled at that too.[1])

> "Testing various options, usually making some wrong turns along the way, ultimately gets ambitious professionals on the road to applying their surest abilities."

What Dryden demonstrates is that when you home in on what you revel in and are good at instead of going after something you're not really wired for, you will be more effective. By trying out all team positions, athletes arrive through trial and error at the position that best fits them. Similarly, medical doctors do several rotations during residency to land on the specialty that

[1] Wikipedia contributors, "Ken Dryden," Wikipedia, February 22, 2024, https://en.wikipedia.org/wiki/Ken_Dryden.

most draws on their unique affinities. Testing various options, usually making some wrong turns along the way, ultimately gets ambitious professionals on the road to applying their surest abilities.

This makes everything less demanding and more gratifying.

That may seem simplistic but it's true. A 40-year study conducted by the Gallup Organization shows that people have "several times more potential for growth when they invest energy in developing their strengths rather than correcting their deficiencies." An even more compelling finding from this research is that people who focus on their strengths at work are "six times more likely to be engaged in their jobs and more than three times as likely to report having an excellent quality of life in general."[2]

If you give it some thought, it's pretty apparent why using your dominant inclinations is such a sure way to simultaneously shine and feel good. The "against the grain" feeling of striving in an area that is not your bailiwick is awkward, whereas doing something you are a natural at, flowing rather than forcing, is affirming. Not to say that using your strengths puts you on easy street—you still have to work at your growth and development even when you're doing what you love—but it sure is a great way to alleviate stress. Just like athletes who train consistently to do well amid colossal competition, you will always be straining to some extent as you achieve at a similarly relentless occupation. However, when you discover and go evermore wholly into your organic leanings, the wind is more present at your back.

> **"Not to say that using your strengths puts you on easy street—you still have to work at your growth and development even when you're doing what you love—but it sure is a great way to alleviate stress."**

It's perfect timing for this chapter because you are now well practiced at the art of considering multiple options, discarding what's not relevant, and capitalizing on what *is* relevant. You are not surprised that defining and exercising your strengths will be about taking in the full picture, narrowing

---

[2] "Our Philosophy," Transforming Strengths, September 23, 2021, http://www.transformingstrengths.com/our-philosophy/#:~:text=Why%20StrengthsFinder%3F,quality%20of%20life%20in%20general.

down, sampling, and settling on what meshes for you. Also, you're pretty sure that going in the direction of your innate disposition, moving further toward doing your best, will give your work and life more of the sense of order and command you want.

I'm going to take you through some exercises for tapping into your assets. First, though, some preliminary background:

Strengths-based working and living is a relatively new offshoot of positive psychology, which, as we've covered, looks at what makes people happy and successful. This focus on strengths is becoming increasingly pertinent as our world spews out ever-increasing interference and tumult. The old generalist aim of trying to be proficient at many things when "many things" keeps multiplying is crazy in the making. The new goal of being a specialist, trying to be good at a few things, means less to keep up with and keep track of, and thus more sanity.

The irony of strengths-based actions is that they seem in sync with you, and so they may not stand out to you as significant. We tend to think in our culture that only what's really hard to make happen is worth anything. Our most popular books and movies commemorate people who overcome unbelievable odds to accomplish the impossible. So we have learned from a young age that if it doesn't take true grit to get something done, whatever you achieve is not that noteworthy.

This is like a client of mine who, when applauded for being his firm's best originator, was surprised because "it's really not that complicated; you just have a couple of lunches and get a contract"; or another client who, every time people tell her she has a way with numbers, says, "It's just common sense." What I tell these clients is that, contrary to our ingrained belief, a standout ability does not necessarily need to be built from sheer exertion. Strengths are those proclivities that seem so obvious to us, we assume everyone must be as inclined as we are toward them. We shrug off compliments in the areas that feel most compatible because we don't think we deserve the praise.

It takes some time to accept the enormous value of gifts that maybe you didn't know you had or didn't take seriously before. Of course, as with any lawyer-like-an-athlete skill, there will be self-examination and experimentation involved. The great news is that the wealth of options out there for exploring what makes you exceptional—easily searchable how-to videos, podcasts, Facebook groups, courses, and so on—makes it possible to refine your particular penchants no matter how obscure they are or how far you want to dive into them.

Attorney in Action

Especially self-aware associate Charlie pinpointed what he had a flair for—extracting patterns from complex data, simplifying complicated concepts for clients, and speaking persuasively to opponents—and wanted to pursue these as an attorney. His boss was open to having him do more of what he had a knack for, and Charlie started to feel less stressed and more motivated despite still having to do various attorney tasks he didn't care for. I emphasized that he could add to his enhanced professional satisfaction by also making an effort to do the personal interests calling him: picking his guitar back up, helping to prevent climate change, and taking downhill skiing lessons. By increasing his engagement in outlets that spoke to him, Charlie amplified the greater alignment he was enjoying at work.

> "Doing what agrees with you away from work is just as integral to making you successful as doing what feels most fitting professionally."

Another plus of strengths-based living and working is that, just like our new hybrid world, it's all integrated. This means that doing what agrees with you away from work is just as integral to making you successful as doing what feels most fitting professionally. So, even if you're in a job that doesn't capitalize on your strengths, engaging in personal pastimes that click for you will contribute to an overall sense of congruity. Riding the wave of your inclinations—whether you're just hanging around with your friends or lawyering—always elevates you.

Charlie's example illustrates well that being in your element, both professionally *and* in your off hours, is the pathway to contentment. What it comes down to is creating a combined sense of ease, stimulation, facility, and pleasure.

With that understanding, you are ready to gain insight into your assets by responding to the questions and prompts below, starting with work:

What do you most enjoy about your job?

____

____

____

What skills do you get the most positive feedback about?

What professional topic do you most want to learn more about?

If you could add something to your job to make it more enjoyable, what would that be?

Is there anything you miss doing from a prior job?

What is your dream position as an attorney?

Review your answers so far, and list any strengths—what you're good at and enjoy doing—that come through for you:

Now, let's look into personal outlets that might further your work satisfaction:

What would you get up early and stay up late to do?

Life is incomplete without:

____

____

____

There's nothing like:

____

____

____

I feel most alive when:

____

____

____

I could ____________________ for hours, and it would feel like time was not passing.

I feel most like me when:

____

____

____

If I had more free time I would:

____

____

____

If I didn't have to worry about money, I would:

____

____

____

I am most curious about:

____

____

____

Next, to make sure you're not missing anything, let's excavate your childhood for clues. Whatever you found interesting and gratifying back then may still appeal to you today. There's nothing like childlike spontaneity, laughter, and playfulness to make the adult world less heavy on your shoulders.

When you were a kid . . .

Who were your favorite people (real and fictional)?

What were your favorite TV shows?

What were your favorite books?

What were your favorite toys/games?

What were your biggest goals?

What made you laugh?

What do you wish you hadn't stopped doing and why?

If you could go back, what would you do differently with interests and goals?

What aspects of that kid are still alive in you today?

Now that you've answered all those questions, step back, consider your responses, and take them all in. You may want to take a little break at this point because you've done a lot here. When you're ready, let's narrow down what you would love to do more of if given the chance.

Don't worry about any obstacles—no time, no room in your schedule—that might interfere. We'll address all that later. For now, just imagine you don't have any roadblocks to deal with.

What might you want to do more of at work to be better aligned with your strengths?

What might you want to do more of away from work to be better in tune with yourself?

Attorney in Action

Devoted attorney Brooke was overextended from being adept at too many things. Whenever she felt stuck doing something just because she was good at it, she would put on a plucky face and get the job done. However, her reputation for being capable across the board was starting to wear on her. Once she took a frank look into herself, she realized that she could feel less frazzled by centering on fewer duties. She made it a rule to, whenever possible, delegate assignments that were not really her thing and prioritize what she was more invested in. By getting better at editing contracts, which she loved to do, she was soon regarded as her firm's editing expert and found herself joining forces with others at work who could excel in areas that didn't interest her.

Now it's time to identify what you can let go of so that you can do more of what rings true for you. Before moving on, though, there are three points you'll want to take into account:

Collaboration is key. Getting back to the precise skills of a hockey goalie, we produce better results when we work together, each of us contributing our distinct strengths to get a collective job done. So, divvy up responsibilities at home and work according to preference whenever that's feasible. A big benefit of organizing a team effort around the exceptional contribution each member brings, rather than distributing responsibility according to gender, seniority, or other unhelpful labels, is that there is also greater diversity, inclusion, and equity, which enhances camaraderie.

Mind the strengths trap. You likely get complimented on abilities specific to you because they attract attention from others who admire them. Though it is always nice to be noticed in this way, strengths count as strengths only if you feel good applying them. So, even if you're the best writer or litigator at work or the best cook or picker-upper at home, you should try to reduce those activities if they're not striking a chord with you, especially if you're doing too much of those things for others.

Be a realist. Even when you are doing work that completely satisfies your soul, there will be aspects to your job that you don't like doing. Same

> "Even when you are doing work that completely satisfies your soul, there will be aspects to your job that you don't like doing. Same at home."

at home. There are adult tasks that even the wealthiest can't unload. The idea here is not to free yourself of all responsibility but to make adjustments where you can by doing less of what you're not into and more of what you are into. Sometimes there are things no one really wants to do, perhaps dealing with some form of tedious bureaucracy at work or taking out the trash at home, and it's a matter of dividing these tasks according to who is less opposed than others to what is distasteful to all. (For example, you might agree to do the dishes at home because you don't mind that chore as much as your spouse does; in return, they might agree to take on the weekly grocery shopping because they don't dislike going to the supermarket as much as you do.)

With those tips in mind, let's continue.

At work:

Are there lawyer skills you'd like to let go of? If so, how can you do fewer of these things?

____

____

____

What can you delegate at work to free up time for your strengths?

____

____

____

What strengths do your work teammates bring to the table?

____

____

____

How do those strengths complement your strengths?

____

____

____

How might you combine proficiencies on your work team to get better results?

____

____

____

How can you reach a better compromise on a work task that no one wants to do?

____

____

____

At home:

Are there home responsibilities you'd rather not handle? If so, how can you do fewer of these things?

____

____

____

What strengths do your companions at home bring to the table?

____

____

____

How do those strengths complement your strengths?

____

____

____

Attorney in Action

Third-year associate Kerry sought coaching because she was disenchanted with her job and wasn't sure why. She'd set up her career to avoid the courtroom because she'd heard how stressful litigation could be, but she was beginning to realize that she was most motivated when she was standing in front of a judge. Through our discussions and some experimentation on her part, she discovered that she wanted to go to court more often. She arranged with her boss to argue more cases, which added to her work satisfaction. It turned out she was instinctively great at being in a high-conflict setting; while her peers found court intimidating, she found it exhilarating. Once she figured this out, we landed on other things that felt more right to her: swimming laps instead of kickboxing, fantasy football instead of playing cribbage, gardening instead of mowing the lawn. The more she organized work and life around her likings, the better she felt, and the more her performance stood out.

How might you combine proficiencies at home to get better results?

____

____

____

How can you reach a better compromise on a home task that no one wants to do?

____

____

____

We're ready now for some tiny steps. As always, remember to take an incremental approach. Just let your leanings guide you, and the more manageable the steps, the better:

Identify three tiny steps you can take to be more aligned with your strengths at work: (For example, you might Google continuing legal education [CLE] webinars on an aspect of law you're wondering about, brainstorm with a close colleague, or cancel an obligatory meeting that you don't really need to attend.)

1. ______________________________
2. ______________________________
3. ______________________________

Identify three tiny steps you can take to be more aligned with your strengths at home: (For example, browse supplies at an art store, discuss the strengths-based approach to chores with your roommate, look into a dinner delivery service so you can cook less.)

1. ______________________________
2. ______________________________
3. ______________________________

As you become more committed to living in line with your tastes and inclinations, you may encounter things in need of revision that you're not ready to deal with yet. If something seems too daunting, then scale it back a bit. If you think it's not just your professional role but your whole career you want to change, or you're thinking other big aspects of your life might need overhauling, just slow down and do what you can at the moment to apply your favored aptitudes just a little bit more in the situations you're in. If you practice greeting every day with the intention to do whatever it is that allows you to relax into what comes genuinely, you will begin to enjoy taking cues from yourself. The next chapter will help you to stay excited and energized as you build on the strengths you've revealed.

"If you practice greeting every day with the intention to do whatever it is that allows you to relax into what comes naturally, you will begin to enjoy taking cues from yourself."

10

Ready, Set, Reset

This topic we're about to enter is where I see the most disagreement among lawyers. There are the stalwart old-schoolers who, completely defying common sense, insist they will be successful in law by working relentlessly without regard for their well-being. Deprived of self-care and life away from lawyering, they rack up physical ailments and personal problems, and then ask why their work seems harder than it used to be. My client Aiden, an eager lawyer launching his career, encountered this antiquated approach when he joined a firm that believed competent lawyers don't let anything come between them and the job. His older colleagues ridiculed him when he said, after two all-nighters holed up in a hotel with them, subsisting on liquor and takeout as they banged away on an out-of-town case, that they couldn't expect him to be in top mental form if he wasn't sleeping.

Then there's the other side of it, the attorneys who see what Aiden sees and are making healthier decisions and encouraging fellow attorneys to do the same. My client Daphne was as astounded as I was delighted when her boss not only encouraged her going on a two-week European cruise but told her that under no circumstances was she to be in contact with her office during that time away. These enlightened lawyers have no interest in behaving in those damaging ways of the old guard and are sitting on attorney wellness committees, modeling the change they want to see, and disrupting dysfunctional patterns in themselves and others whenever they have that power.

You're over halfway through this book now, and so if you're practicing the principles persistently enough to be seeing some agreeable outcomes, you are one of those informed attorneys I'm talking about. You are definitely ready to zero in on what is arguably the most lifesaving, soul-nourishing lesson attorneys can learn from athletes:

The lesson is this:

Too little stress = boredom, apathy, stilted motivation

Too much stress = exhaustion, sickness, injury

Manageable stress = achievement, resilience, good spirits

Psychologists talk about two types of stress. There's distress, which is what we encounter when we are overwhelmed and not prepared to cope with stressors, such as being placed in a work position without sufficient training. And then there's eustress, which we experience when we are equipped to handle stressors well. An example of eustress is being amped up to study hard for an important exam commensurate with your academic ranking. Stress will always be part of life, and it's a matter of finding that sweet spot where stress is rousing rather than sabotaging.

More clearly in athlete terms, having the right amount of fire under you is integral to winning. Structured training is conducted in stages that incrementally push your mental and physical limits, and the adrenaline and excitement of that challenge is what keeps you focused on performance goals. If there's insufficient structure and the end goal isn't compelling enough, progress will be uninspired and sluggish. If there is too much pressure to get somewhere fast, the mind and muscles can break down and give out.

That's what happens in the movie *The Wrestler*,[1] where an aging professional wrestler riddled with horribly defeating habits and zero self-respect drives his wrestling and his life into the ground through his win-at-all-costs approach. There is no breaking away to counteract the stress, and so the stress ultimately wins.

As athletic coach Sage Rountree says, "Endurance sports are about testing the limits. You work your body to a breaking point, then step away from the brink, let the work absorb, and repeat."[2] Similar to athletes, you must prioritize replenishing intermissions to consistently function in ways

---

[1] *The Wrestler*, directed by Darren Aronofsky (Fox Searchlight Pictures, 2008), https://en.wikipedia.org/wiki/The_Wrestler_(2008_film).

[2] Sage Rountree, *The Athlete's Guide to Recovery: Rest, Relax, and Restore for Peak Performance* (Rowman & Littlefield Publishers, 2024).

that make you competitive in your strenuous field. Overuse your assets and you lose your edge.

> "Similar to athletes, you must prioritize replenishing intermissions to consistently function in ways that make you competitive in your strenuous field. Overuse your assets and you lose your edge."

Now, here's where you need to incorporate breaks if you want to lawyer like an athlete:

Reset between work sessions: Just like muscles need rest between physical workouts to come back stronger, you need respite from mental exertion to return to your work with renewed vigor. Since research precisely shows that "humans naturally move from full focus and energy to physiological fatigue every 90 minutes," it's a good general practice to take a five-minute break every hour-and-a-half.[3] I want to emphasize that word "break," as in "breaking away": actually getting up, walking around, doing something altogether different from the work you're putting aside. Maybe stand up and reach your arms as high as you can, refill your water bottle, or grab a healthful snack. Better yet, go outside, look up at the sky, absorb the air around you, take in whatever greenery you see. Being outdoors, just for a few minutes, even in the middle of an urban environment, is the most potent way to ready yourself for your next 90-minute round—especially if you are working in front of a screen.

Reset at midday: A mini-break every 90 minutes isn't enough if you're working all day. A lunch break is essential, too, so that you can let your body and brain enjoy some diversion. Taking enough midday time out to fortify yourself with a meal, perhaps tending to your personal to-do list, or maybe taking a short walk will ready you for a productive afternoon. Even more preferable is enjoying lunch with a friend or colleague since that's an excellent contribution to the nourishing relationships portion of the work-plus model.

---

[3] Ibid.

Attorney in Action

Amir, a new associate at a personal injury firm, realized the importance of self-care from attending a progressive law school. He came to coaching because he didn't feel supported in taking work breaks when none of his coworkers seemed to realize the value of rest and recovery. I suggested that he research attorney wellness initiatives in his state and get involved with one so that he could have some company. By participating in a group that advocated for lawyer well-being, Amir was not only able to feel validated as he strove to keep his stress at a healthy level; he also had some impact on his firm by sharing what he was learning.

Reset after work: We went over this in Chapter 4, and I'm bringing it up again because it's so critical. Your evening should be about unspooling your thoughts and taking the load off, then getting enough sleep to wake up refreshed. Don't be tempted to prep for a case or answer work emails. You're in charge of this reset, so use your time wisely to relax.

Weekly reset: You're learning through this book to take back time in all areas of your life and work by eliminating what doesn't warrant or deserve your attention. Now with time freed up that you didn't know you had, you are ready to take back your weekends. Using Saturday and Sunday for what they are intended means rewarding yourself for getting through another work week. Weekends are your opportunity to get away from your Monday-through-Friday routine and do what is restful, enlivening, and contrasting. Depending on the week you just finished, you might want to revel in solitude, observe a special occasion, catch up on news, take a nap, visit a museum, check out a new restaurant, get your hair cut, socialize with loved ones, tackle a domestic project, or play a sport. Mix your weekends up in whatever ways appeal to you. Make sure to go on a day trip or weekend away once in a while so that you can treat yourself to a change of venue.

Annual reset: From my experience, attorneys who take a bona fide vacation—two weeks away from home with no work—every year are more successful than other attorneys all the way around. So, if you're thinking right now that you're too busy for a vacation, think again, because not taking vacations is a bad move professionally and personally. Recovery periods throughout your workday, after your workday, and on weekends will absolutely help you to be happier and healthier and more dynamic, but it's the *annual* recovery that takes your well-being and performance to a whole new level.

Vacations done right—again, that's two full weeks away from home, no working—are incredibly powerful because they give you sufficient time to decompress, downshift, and function at a restorative rhythm. One of the biggest advantages of an annual vacation is that you get enough distance from your life and work to broaden your point of view. Between the fun, leisure, and exposure to novel vistas, your at-home thinking patterns get disrupted, and new insights and epiphanies emerge. My client Daphne who went on that cruise vacation returned to work not only with renewed enthusiasm but with some great ideas that her boss loved, and she attributes that to being untethered from work for two full weeks.

> "Always having an enticing reset to look forward to, knowing there really is some kind of end in sight, makes it easier to get through even the most demanding workdays."

To ensure that resets happen, it's important to book them into your schedule. What's cool about that is the

Attorney in Action

Isabella, an overextended criminal attorney, totally got that she needed resets when she started coaching with me, but she felt overrun by her schedule and didn't know how she could work them in. I suggested that we use a session just to look at her calendar, plan ahead, and gradually incorporate break time. By experimenting between sessions and continuing to rework her calendar with me, Isabella eventually arrived at a realistic schedule, and she found that taking breaks seriously enough to make them an official part of her job made them seem much more official and possible.

more alluring an upcoming break is to you, the more motivated you will be as you work your way up to it. Whether it's an afternoon indulgence or a trip abroad, make your recovery plans tempting enough to keep you on task and engaged. Always having an enticing reset to look forward to, knowing there really is some kind of end in sight, makes it easier to get through even the most taxing workdays.

WHAT MIGHT YOUR RESET CALENDAR LOOK LIKE?

You can start fleshing ideas out by answering the questions below:

What are three things you can do on a five-minute break from work?

1. ____________________
2. ____________________
3. ____________________

How can you fill an hour-long lunch break to promote a fruitful and satisfying afternoon?

____

____

____

How's your evening routine going? Anything you want to do differently?

____

____

____

How's your sleep? Anything you want to improve there?

____

____

____

What does an ideal Saturday look like?

____

____

____

What appeals to you for a day trip?

____

____

____

Where would you most like to go for a weekend trip?

____

____

____

What sounds good for a two-week vacation?

____

____

____

After you've answered these questions, I want you to get some real-time practice by taking an interlude from this chapter. You've just given credence to ideas you have for covering all the reset bases we've gone over. Now, put this book down and go do something else to allow your best ideas to formulate. When you're ready, come back and home in on the reset ideas you most want to test out.

LIST THREE TINY STEPS YOU CAN TAKE TO:

Incorporate breaks into your workday:

1. ______________________________________
2. ______________________________________
3. ______________________________________

Get away from it all on weekends:

1. ______________________________________
2. ______________________________________
3. ______________________________________

Enjoy a two-week vacation:

1. ____________________
2. ____________________
3. ____________________

Now, some important points before you put your recovery plan into motion:

Don't rely on reset cramming. When you don't mix in resets regularly and attempt to undo your exhaustion by sleeping all weekend or finally taking a vacation, you don't get the benefit. For resets to make any kind of lasting impact, they must happen on all the levels we've covered on an ongoing basis. While you may feel temporarily revived when you take occasional time off to intensely recuperate, you will go right back to overwhelming yourself if you don't return to a full reset schedule where you integrate breaks into your day, week, month, and year.

"While you may feel temporarily revived when you take occasional time off to intensely recuperate, you will go right back to overwhelming yourself if you don't return to a full reset schedule where you integrate breaks into your day, week, month, and year."

Attorney in Action

Eli, a longtime partner at an established firm, came to coaching because his fellow partners were concerned that he was burning out. He attributed his work success to eating while working, putting in hours at night and on weekends, and working while his family vacationed, but he was willing to consider that his all-work, no-break policy might be serving him less as he got older. Though he was willing to try the reset thing, he was afraid that rest and recovery, even in five-minute increments, would interfere with his belief that he should be working at the beck and call of his clients. By getting used to the idea of breaks little by little, session by session, he was able to see that, to his surprise, withdrawing regularly from work actually made him better able to be more present and patient with his clients and solve problems more swiftly for them.

Don't fool yourself. Attorneys often tell me they don't take breaks during the day because they don't want to interrupt "being in the zone." What these attorneys don't realize is that there is a point where "being in the zone" shifts from being really tuned in to being dazed and bleary-eyed. Remember what the studies tell us: if you're working beyond 90-minute periods without breaking away, you are depleting yourself and risking turning in low-quality work.

Be flexible: My general reset parameters are based on a traditional nine-to-five schedule, which may not fit your time frame. If you're self-employed, working from home, traveling a lot, or working part-time, you'll want to make adjustments. For example, if you prefer working on Saturdays because it's easier to avoid interruptions, then substitute a weekday for that weekend day you are missing. If you have a schedule that doesn't permit taking a break every 90 minutes, try to get as close to that as you can. Lawyer-like-an-athlete principles are most effective when you adapt them to your real life.

Don't expect flawlessness: You can best work in my rest-and-recovery rules by allowing for inevitable uncertainty to intervene. Deadlines will sometimes prevent you from taking breaks from intense work every 90 minutes. You may have to work some nights and weekends and on vacations no matter how well you plan. As with everything else you're learning from this book, success is a matter of doing the right things *most* of the time, *not all* of the time.

At the conclusion of this chapter, I expect you're not totally sold on this reset thing, especially two whole weeks away from your job every year—because there aren't a lot of lawyers who admire lawyers who take breaks. While the party line is that workaholic lawyers are actually brave warriors who keep up the fight no matter what, the truth is that the real heroes in law are those who are courageous enough to defy that destructive mindset. Ryan Hall, holder of the American half-marathon record, concurs. "I constantly remind myself that resting takes confidence. Anyone can train like a madman but to embrace rest and to allow all the hard training to come out takes mental strength."[4]

---

[4] "Ryan Hall Quotes," Love Expands, n.d., https://loveexpands.com/quotes/ryan-hall-752691/.

What's critical to keep in mind right now is that you'll have to take a lot of small risks outside your comfort zone before you see that taking breaks is actually a good idea. It will take returning to your work from breaks often enough to see that your clients haven't gone down the street, your work hasn't dried up, you are not disposable, and, more important, you are actually a more sought-after attorney for taking those regular intermissions.

As you're facing your fears and applying your own mental strength to put resets on your calendar and follow through with them, you can look forward to what's in store. The next chapter introduces a performance-enhancing activity you can practice during recess from work, and you'll learn to intentionally boost your success in a manner that is quite relaxing.

11

Rehearse Your Wins

Picture right now something you do regularly as part of being an attorney that you really don't like doing. Is it meeting with distressed clients, making a dent in paperwork, configuring technology, or keeping track of your billable hours? Now picture yourself at home, same unlikeable task: power-washing the house, planning meals for your week, cleaning up, anything you'd rather not be doing. Whatever it is, whether at work or home, notice the thoughts and feelings that arise from envisioning yourself doing something you're not crazy about. Whatever unsavory images you're calling up, your resulting thoughts may conjure feelings of tedium, frustration, fatigue, and tension.

Not exactly motivating.

Now imagine that unavoidable home or work activity you don't care for again—only this time imagine you are actually *not* feeling bothered by it. What thoughts and feelings arise when you are doing the same thing with less resistance? Probably some semblance of engagement, aliveness, interest, or confidence—some of what you know you need to lawyer like an athlete.

That's motivating.

As you've been seeing, your inner experience is enormously impactful. You are aware that improving the quality of your interior world, rather than trying to control things outside of you, is how to maximize your influence. Now, with your perspective enhanced enough to acquire the skill, you are ready to access an underused and quite powerful chamber of your mind.

"When you blend into the preparation visualizing things going well, seeing scenarios as you want them to unfold, and mentally rehearsing your way to an appealing outcome, you are likely to achieve desired results with greater ease."

I call it going to your visualization workshop, and it goes like this:

Virtually every major athlete operates from the rule that things are apt to go more smoothly and in their favor when they pave the way internally for what they want to occur. When you worry about and dread events, replaying the motions of the worst-case scenarios, you are more likely to be stressed and not do very well—even when you are objectively fit for the task. However, when you blend into the preparation visualizing things going well, seeing scenarios as you want them to unfold, and mentally rehearsing your way to an appealing outcome, you are likely to achieve desired results with greater ease.

Prominent sports psychology researchers Drs. Deborah Feltz and Daniel Landers describe visualization as "one of the most powerful performance weapons we have in our mental arsenal."[1] Mental rehearsal is so potent because the neurocircuitry of physical performance is strengthened not just by actual movement but also by running through the motions of performance beforehand. As we've covered in past chapters, a positive inside experience is more likely to attract a positive outside experience. Albert Einstein said it in this intriguing way: "Everything is energy and that's all there is to it. Match the frequency of the reality you want and you cannot help but get that reality. It can be no other way."[2]

One of my favorite examples of visualization in sports is when champion diver Laura Wilkinson got sidelined by a foot injury six months before the 2000 Olympics. Though she wasn't able to train, she spent significant time every day doing her training routines in her head. The remarkable thing is that she healed enough to participate in the Olympics

---

[1] Jim Afremow, *The Champion's Mind: How Great Athletes Think, Train, and Thrive* (Pennsylvania: Rodale Books, 2013), 34.

[2] Quoteresearch, "Everything Is Energy and That's All There Is to It. Match the Frequency of the Reality You Want," May 16, 2012, https://quoteinvestigator.com/2012/05/16/everything-energy/.

and was on par with her competitors—despite having done far less physical preparation.[3]

Then there's the striking visualization story about Michael Phelps, whose pre-2008 Olympics visualization ritual included every aspect of winning, from diving in the pool to navigating unexpected obstacles to celebrating. Because his mental rehearsing had included swimming in the dark during a power failure, he was unfazed when an unforeseen leak in his goggles fogged his vision during a race—and he got the gold anyway.[4]

So instrumental is visualization to achievement in sports that it is considered a standard and vital part of winning. This advanced means of reducing resistance is just as integral for attorneys, who must access every inner resource to stay competitive. Choreographing in your head what you want to have happen, creating and directing the script, will prompt you forward. Says Canadian bobsledder Lyndon Rush about the role visualizing played in training for the Olympics: "I've tried to keep the track in my mind throughout the year. I'll be in the shower or brushing my teeth. It just takes a minute, so I do the whole thing or sometimes just the corners that are more technical. You try to keep it fresh in your head, so when you do get there, you are not just starting at square one. It's amazing how much you can do in your mind."[5]

"So instrumental is visualization to achievement in sports that it is considered a standard and vital part of winning. This advanced means of reducing resistance is just as integral for attorneys."

There is no guarantee, of course, that you will get everything you want, but being at your best is more possible when you have programmed your brain for it.

---

[3] Wikipedia contributors, "Laura Wilkinson," Wikipedia, March 6, 2024, https://en.wikipedia.org/wiki/Laura_Wilkinson.

[4] Adarsh Srinivas Reddy, "Michael Phelps and his Blind Swimming in the Olympics," LinkedIn, August 4, 2020, https://www.linkedin.com/pulse/michael-phelps-his-blind-swimming-olympics-adarsh-s/.

[5] Patrick Cohn, "Sports Visualization: The Secret Weapon of Athletes," Peak Performance Sports, n.d., https://www.peaksports.com/sports-psychology-blog/sports-visualization-athletes/.

Attorney in Action

Cash, a veteran lawyer at his family's three-generation firm, had learned from coaching that he needed to reduce his work hours if he wanted to be less tired and more efficient. The problem was his colleagues—family he'd worked with for years—equated his coming in later and leaving earlier with being less committed, and it was hard to ignore their disapproving looks. By visualizing himself standing firm in the face of judgment, performing better than ever due to his smarter schedule, Cash was able to persist with his new behavior. Though it took a while, his family eventually saw that his dedication to the firm was renewed from taking better care of himself.

> "The secret to effective visualization is to create a crystal-clear image of how you would respond to any outcome."

The secret to effective visualization is to create a crystal-clear image of how you would respond to any outcome. By bringing in sights, sounds, smells, tactile impressions, and emotions, you capture the total performance experience. Don't just picture the finished stack of contracts; imagine yourself confidently writing them, savoring the invigorating sensation of water hydrating you, feeling poised by the perfect temperature of your office. A snapshot of you smiling as a know-it-all client tells you how to practice law is fine, but you'll get more momentum if you pull in your calming pulse, unflustered patience, and the soothing light-aqua paint color on your office walls. Steve Backley, record-holder for javelin throwing, describes productive visualization as "building high-definition videos in your mind's eye of exactly what you are trying to achieve."[6]

Now, how about trying some visualization?

6 Jim Afremow, *The Champion's Mind: How Great Athletes Think, Train, and Thrive* (Pennsylvania: Rodale Books, 2013), 36.

IMAGINE WHAT YOU'D LIKE THIS EVENING TO BE LIKE:

Describe yourself enjoying your evening.

What are you seeing?

What are you hearing?

What are you thinking?

What are you feeling?

What sensations are you experiencing in your body?

Now, let's try this at work:

Imagine how you'd like your workday to go:

What are you seeing?

What are you hearing?

____

____

____

What are you thinking?

____

____

____

What are you feeling?

____

____

____

What sensations are you experiencing in your body?

____

____

____

Try visualizing these scenarios for about five minutes per day over the next week or so, and see what happens from your rehearsal, making adjustments as you go, getting ever more vivid.

Write any notes here:

____

____

____

____

What I love about visualization is there are so many ways to go at it, and, like I said, it's entertaining.

I'll give you more strategies soon, but first some visualization pointers:

Apply the tiny-step rule: Visualization is more productive when you're imagining desired results that are just far enough out of reach to light that necessary fire under you, and not so ahead of where you are now that they frighten you. If you have never exercised before and you want to get in shape, you'll want to imagine yourself enjoying walks around a nearby park rather than winning a marathon. Likewise, if you are trying to be more at ease with cross-examination, you might start by picturing yourself waking up on a workday with a settled stomach instead of totally nailing your question. Once you successfully accomplish the tiny step you've been mentally rehearsing, you can move on to your next tiny step and next tiny step, and so on.

Make it about you: We've established that other people can't be controlled, and no amount of visualization can make other people do what you want them to do. The most productive visualizing comes from you imagining yourself doing, feeling, and sensing what *you* want for yourself. So, if your teenager is struggling academically and they're not trying to do better, visualizing them as high school valedictorian is not going to help. If your boss is a jerk, visualizing them being nice to you is not going to make a difference. In both cases, it would make more sense to visualize yourself being less reactive and more grounded amid circumstances you can't force.

Visualization alone is not enough: I've already said this and it's worth repeating: success comes from a combination of visualization *and* action. There is a lot of misinformation out there about visualization accomplishing miracles; just picture what you want and it will manifest. In a culture always looking for quick fixes, this approach

Attorney in Action

Susanne, a lawyer specializing in child custody cases, came to coaching to feel less disrupted in the face of sudden changes at work, particularly emergency hearings. She was so unnerved by constantly shifting priorities that her anxiety was chronic, and she was on hyperalert all the time. Though she couldn't dictate when urgent matters erupted during her workday, Susanne learned that she could be less frazzled by envisioning herself responding less frantically. By imagining herself being steadily more agile when confronted with change, she became better able to handle the unexpected at work and everywhere else too.

is seductive, but it doesn't really amount to much. Unless you are making an effort to accomplish the things you are imagining, you are unlikely to get good results.

Here's another exercise: Imagine it's one year from now and you have gained what you wanted from reading this book. Picture yourself as happier, more productive, and feeling excited about getting to a better place.

NOW, LET THAT MORE SUCCESSFUL *FUTURE YOU* ANSWER THESE QUESTIONS:

What component of the work-plus model—exquisite self-care, grounded perspective, nourishing diversions, thriving relationships—do you see most improvement in?

____

____

____

What bad habit have you given up?

____

____

____

How has your health improved?

____

____

____

What is the most positive change in your social world?

____

____

____

What positive feedback do you most get?

____

____

____

What three things are going better at work?

____

____

____

How do you spend your free time?

____

____

____

Where are you going on your next vacation?

____

____

____

Now, review all your answers and you'll see that your responses give you a sketch of what it looks and feels like to lawyer like an athlete. What you have here is essentially a blueprint that can inform your goals and tiny steps.

This next exercise will refine that blueprint further.

YOUR LIFE AS A MOVIE

Imagine it is one year from now and you have become more successful in the ways that are most meaningful to you. A documentary has been made about your success. Five pivotal scenes—your outcomes realized—are featured in the movie trailer. Possible scenes could include leaving your office at 5 p.m. feeling satisfied, laughing with a friend you have more time for, hearing your doctor affirm you for eating better and losing weight, or responding calmly to a challenging colleague—whatever vignettes will powerfully convey the essence of how far you've come.

List your pivotal scenes here:

1. ____
2. ____
3. ____

4. ______________________________
5. ______________________________

Now, read those movie scenes over and see what occurs to you. Based on where you are now, is the image of yourself one year from now a reasonable goal? If not, adjust the scenes to make them realistic.

Next, keeping in mind that action is part of the visualization formula, let's narrow down some tiny steps you can take over the next year to implement the four components of the work-plus model:

Where do you want to be with self-care one year from now?

____

____

____

Three tiny steps you can take to get moving in that direction:

1. ______________________________
2. ______________________________
3. ______________________________

Where do you want to be with your perspective one year from now?

____

____

____

Three tiny steps you can take to get moving in that direction:

1. ______________________________
2. ______________________________
3. ______________________________

What nourishing diversions do you want to be participating in one year from now?

____

____

____

Three tiny steps you can take to get moving in that direction:

1. ______________________________
2. ______________________________
3. ______________________________

Where do you want to be with your relationships one year from now?

____

____

____

Three tiny steps you can take to get moving in that direction:

1. ______________________________
2. ______________________________
3. ______________________________

Just from carrying out the assignments of this chapter, you are experiencing the heart of how visualization works. When you imagine yourself doing well, you are bringing up undeniably real positive feelings and thoughts. As you consequently feel better in the present, you will be more hopeful, less doubting, as you take on hurdles in the future.

As always, I encourage you to close this book for a bit, give yourself some time to believe more fully in the power of making things up. When you're ready, we'll move into the third part of your lawyer-like-an-athlete training, which is all about staying on course with everything you've learned and taking it further—no matter what the obstacle or how heated the moment.

"When you imagine yourself doing well, you are bringing up undeniably real positive feelings and thoughts. As you consequently feel better in the present, you will be more hopeful, less doubting, as you take on hurdles in the future."

STAGE THREE

Playoffs

12

Power Through

Brittney Griner is an unbelievably exemplary athlete and not just because she has reached Olympian and NBA heights in basketball. Brittney also stands out because she has risen to some tough occasions: overcoming an anger problem that led to domestic violence charges, being the first openly gay Nike sponsor, and surviving the nightmare of being falsely imprisoned for carrying prescribed medicinal cannabis into Russia.[1] However, what really makes Brittney exceptional is that she faces such challenges squarely, handles adversity with aplomb, recovers (there's that word again), and then gets fully back to the game.

Ultimately, what Brittney does brilliantly is manage her inner resources well. She knows that her reserves have a limit and channels them into what seems most worthwhile. So, while it would be perfectly understandable, given the extremes she has endured, for her to be jaded, angry, and wallowing rather than winning, she would rather put her energy into transcending seemingly unfair hardship and getting on with things. She truly honors her own energy supply by getting the best she can from it, and in turn her energy gives back by helping her sustain excellence in her sport and life.

Every athlete can learn from Brittney Griner, and so can you.

First, a little energy primer:

Energy is currency. We each have a finite amount of it, and those amounts vary. There are countless ways to disburse our energy, and we

---

[1] Wikipedia contributors, "Brittney Griner," Wikipedia, April 5, 2024, https://en.wikipedia.org/wiki/Brittney_Griner.

often throw it away by spending it foolishly. The quality of our existence is directly proportional to our discernment in spending our energy wisely.

Allocating energy foolishly results in reacting impulsively, moving about without intention or purpose, allowing temptation and temper to take the lead, and before you know it, you're depleted and unhappy.

"Expending energy wisely leads to responding thoughtfully, with a mix of intuition and pragmatic control, so that you are fulfilled and fortified and can say at the end of the day that you like what you did with it, all things considered."

Expending energy wisely leads to responding thoughtfully, with a mix of intuition and pragmatic control, so that you are fulfilled and fortified and can say at the end of the day that you like what you did with it, all things considered.

By this stage of the book, you should already be seeing the perks of using your energy prudently. You are likely planning and prioritizing better, eating and exercising sufficiently, resting and sleeping more, managing distractions with more agility, being clear with your boundaries, surrounding yourself with positive people, and doing all sorts of other lawyer-like--an-athlete things that are giving you greater vitality.

Even though you may have many of the essentials of my program down, you still may not be using your energy as judiciously as you could be. Remember, you're no ordinary professional; you're an attorney who will be continually tested, and you need to make sure you're getting the full value of your energy as you navigate each trial—literally and figuratively—especially on those particularly relentless days when the effort required is bigger than usual. Think of this energy chapter as looking closer to make sure there are no cracks that might let cold air get in and compromise your heating system.

Concentrating your energy more shrewdly starts with three central questions:

- *How much energy do you have?*
- *What do you want to put your limited energy into?*
- *How can you maximize your energy so that you have more resources for what you want to do and still deal with the inevitable, unexpected/uncontrollable obstacles?*

Let's start with determining how much energy you have.

As you live the lawyer-like-an-athlete philosophy, striving to practice exquisite self-care, a grounded perspective, nourishing diversions, and healthy relationships, take the following self-inventory:

Where are you on the continuum between feeling in charge and being outdone on an average day?

In charge ________________________ Outdone

Where are you between feeling satisfied and experiencing exhaustion at the end of your average day?

Satisfied ________________________ Exhausted

If you're closer to feeling in charge and satisfied, you are directing your energy pretty responsibly. If you are leaning more toward the outdone/exhausted side, you probably don't have enough energy for what you're taking on. Either way, it's always smart to find ways to increase your energy because you can never be too good at capitalizing on your most precious resource.

> "It's always smart to find ways to increase your energy because you can never be too good at capitalizing on your most precious resource."

The first step to increasing your energy is determining what is depleting you.

What do you find to be most draining for you at work?

____

____

____

What do you find to be most draining for you in your personal life?

____

____

____

In what ways are people asking too much of you?

____

____

____

In what ways are bad habits robbing your energy?

____

____

____

In what ways are you wasting energy by dwelling on or stewing about anything?

____

____

____

In what other ways are you throwing energy currency out the window?

____

____

____

Once you know how you are misusing your energy, you can make adjustments to each component of the work-plus model. Beyond refining your perspective, relationships, self-care, and pastimes as necessary to give you a lift, these strategies will help you to get more out of the energy you have.

Go with your energy vacillations: Each of us differs not only in the amount of energy we have but in where it goes throughout the year, month, week, and day. Are you a morning person or a night person? A winter person or a summer person? When does your brain work at its best, and when are you more inclined to be resting? Scheduling your most challenging intellectual work when you are feeling sharpest and doing routine tasks when you are not up for peak cognitive performance is the idea here. There will always be times when you will have to do high-energy things when you're feeling low-energy, and you will power through those times more easily if you arrange your calendar to appreciate your unique energy fluctuations whenever you can.

Know what innately boosts your energy: Introverts get energy from being alone, and extroverts get energy from being social. Where do you fall? And are you being true to your introvert or extrovert self? What may be energizing to one person may be sapping to another, so it's important to know your distinctive proclivities here. Maybe you're interacting with upbeat people who for some reason drag you down, or you're participating in activities that are amusing to your friends but just don't do it for you. If it doesn't bring you alive, no matter how much it works for others, it's okay to drop it.

> "If it doesn't bring you alive, no matter how much it works for others, it's okay to drop it."

Attorney in Action

Ben had been in coaching with me long enough to have adopted many new ways of doing things that were making his life and work better. But even though he'd become committed to a more sensible rest-and-renewal schedule, he was feeling resentful about going to bed when he wanted to be awake. He realized that he was a night owl and did his best intellectual work in the middle of the night, so he put his eight hours in between 3:00 a.m. and 11:00 a.m. Fortunately, Ben worked from home and had the flexibility necessary to change his schedule to what suited him better. His partner preferred that they go to bed at the same "reasonable hour," but he got on board when Ben explained to him the importance of keeping to his night owl disposition. Never mind that it wasn't the standard; it worked best for him.

Now that you've seen how Ben aligned his work levels with his energy levels, you'll want to answer these questions:

How can you get more in the flow of your energy fluctuations at home?

____

____

____

How can you get more in the flow of your energy fluctuations at work?

____

____

____

How can you reduce work activities that drain you?

____

____

____

How can you reduce personal activities that drain you?

____

____

____

For those draining work activities you can't change, how can you make them less draining by thinking about them differently?

____

____

____

For those draining personal activities you can't change, how can you make them less draining by thinking about them differently?

____

____

____

Along with funneling your vibrancy better, it's important to know how to boost your energy when you are flagging and yet can't stop for a breather. Think of the marathoner who pops an energy gel pack into their mouth for the final hurdle or the running-on-empty team that leans in for a fourth-quarter pep talk from the coach. You already know the importance of breaks to keep your momentum going, but some days will still outrun you, and you will need quick fuel. Here's how to get that infusion so you can keep going:

Find a way to laugh: Sparking your sense of humor will immediately interrupt your lagging spirit and rouse you. So, just go to whatever it is you find funny: an SNL skit you love, five minutes watching your favorite satirist, or a silly pet video. Or recall your most hilarious memory, think of the most ridiculous thing you've ever seen, or remember a time when you laughed so hard you cried.

Listen to an empowering song: Music that moves you in an upward way is very reviving, and your favorite tunes can immediately bring up buoying thoughts. Keep music at hand to give you a surge of confidence, motivation, delight, or whatever is needed to get you going again. There are all sorts of playlists for this purpose, so curate one for yourself that has the most impact.

Do a brain dump: When your tank is running low, you can improve efficiency by downloading any thoughts that may be leaking away your energy. Just set a timer for five minutes, then type or write without stopping every single thought tumbling out. The effect will be a mind vacuum that sucks out inner distraction and frees up space and sustenance.

Clear off your desk: You are already aware that removing extraneous stuff from your environment is a sure way to feel less stressed, and we're going further with that here. Surpassing standard decluttering, you want to be meticulous about removing from your surroundings what is stealing from rather than adding to your stamina. Even if it's just a stray lunch napkin or an extra pen in your sightline, the energy required to notice it could be used more productively elsewhere. Taking just a minute or two for a clean sweep can refill your well.

Attorney in Action

Meredith started to question coaching when she saw that she was feeling up against the wall at times as a litigator. Though she had come a long way with the work-plus model, she was still dealing with unforeseen, nonnegotiable deadlines that pushed her beyond her energy limit. We landed on a few ways she could keep herself going when she felt out of steam: thinking about her best childhood friend who always knew how to crack her up, singing her high school fight song in her head, writing down five things she is really grateful for, and swiveling more precisely to her next immediate step. When she incorporated emergency energy boosters into her approach, she felt more adequately pumped up when she needed to be.

Snap out of it: When you are drooping and dragging, you can shake up your energy by doing something physically invigorating. Get out of your chair and jump around, breathe in an enlivening scent, or splash cold water on your face and you will feel promptly revived. It's also okay here to gulp down a caffeinated drink as an emergency measure—just recall that this can squelch your energy if it becomes a habit.

Keep your energy in check: Just like you stay current with your bank account online to avoid overdraft fees, it's important to closely monitor your energy to ensure that you don't run out. Your energy can shift with age, biochemistry, goals, and other circumstances, so you need to keep your eye on it and make adjustments when necessary. Yawning may make you realize that you don't have what it takes to stay out with your friends as late as you used to. Being irritated by sounds that never fazed you before could mean that you're developing a preference for quieter locales. Having to psych yourself up for a volunteer activity you used to enjoy may indicate it's time for a new pro bono gig.

As we end this chapter, I want to give you one final way of thinking about energy that will help you put principle into practice.

Imagine that you have a certain frequency that serves you best when you match it to compatible frequencies. Like a radio, the closer the frequency match, the less static. And so, the more you are engaged with

Attorney in Action

Giselle, a longtime copyright attorney, came to coaching because she was finding her job more stressful than usual, even though not much had changed. She had been glad that copyright law had proven to be less intense than other types of law when she went into it years ago, but she was feeling inexplicably under the gun at work. Giselle realized from our discussions that hanging out with a new high-energy neighbor was trying her socially. She also learned from her medical doctor that a minor autoimmune condition was pulling her down. By reducing the time she spent with her neighbor and ordering some recommended nutritional supplements, she was able to get her verve back to where she wanted it.

people and pursuits that seem compatible with your liveliness level, the more in tune you will be. It's a big commitment to continually recognize your varying energy levels, revolve your schedule around those variances, reduce activities that lower your zest without benefit, and address alterations in your energy patterns and cycles. However, because energy is a compounding currency, the more you invest in this process, the more energy you will have. The next chapter will build on your capacity to channel your vigor smartly by delving into what's most worthy of your wherewithal.

> "The more you are engaged with people and pursuits that seem compatible with your energy level, the more in tune you will be."

13

Keep Your Eye on the Prize

Famous professional athletes delight in donating money to natural disaster relief, medical research, animal welfare, and other initiatives aimed at making the world a better place. After all, who doesn't dream of having enough money to give to the less fortunate? Along with meaning well, they need the tax write-offs, and it's good for the brand to be associated with fixing the social problems less-wealthy fans are most concerned about. However, the athletes that really attract attention as exemplary role models are those who surpass standard philanthropy by putting themselves on the line in the name of a cause that is personally significant to them, like former San Francisco 49er Colin Kaepernick, who protested police brutality and other racial issues by kneeling during the US national anthem—despite such negative attention that he was eventually released from his team; or former Cleveland Guardians pitcher Daniel Norris, who lives in a van and spends frugally to rail against overconsumption and materialism. Then there's Georges St-Pierre, the mixed martial arts hero who openly drug-tested while training to demonstrate that success in sports is possible without steroids.[1,2]

What these three famous athletes have in common is allegiance to something greater than a desire to win the game. For them, standing up (or

---

[1] "Five Pro Athletes Who Put Ethics Above Profits," Sports Management Degree Guide, n.d., https://www.sports-management-degrees.com/lists/five-pro-athletes-who-put-ethics-above-profits/.

[2] TS Staff, "Top 15 Athletes Who Are the Best Rolemodels," TheSportster, May 22, 2015, https://www.thesportster.com/entertainment/top-15-athletes-who-are-the-best-rolemodels/.

> "Aspiring to that higher objective, something so personally central to self that not pursuing it would be disingenuous, gives you a shining bright beacon when you're getting lost in the weeds of the repetitive grind and losing sight of the bigger vision."

in Kaepernick's case, kneeling) for what they believe in above all else is the more compelling goal that pulls them forward. Aspiring to that higher objective, something so personally central to self that not pursuing it would be disingenuous, gives them a shining bright beacon when they're getting mired in the weeds of the repetitive grind and losing sight of the bigger vision.

What we're talking about here is values, what you deem most important to you at the end of the day. Values can be modeling what you want to be known for: honesty, morality, humility, courage, and self-respect. Values can be what you strive for with others: connection, collaboration, understanding, creativity, and positivity. Values can be the passions you reward yourself with: travel, entertainment, or adventure. Values can also be your most earnest goals: quality time with family and friends, private schooling for the kids, an in-ground swimming pool, a mountain house one day, or a carefree retirement.

When you keep your eye on your values, regarding them as the most satisfying prize of all prizes, whatever you are doing at the moment becomes more meaningful. Instead of thinking while attacking yet another pile of files, for example, that your career is not getting you anywhere, you can remember that your salary is what's paying to live in a great neighborhood or take a cooking course in France on your next vacation.

> "When you keep your eye on your values, regarding them as the most satisfying prize of all prizes, whatever you are doing at the moment becomes more meaningful."

Seemingly complicated decisions are simplified when you rise above your fears and doubts and define the esteemed characteristics you want to emulate. A temptation to pad your hours or have an affair, for instance, is squashed when you ascent from the emotion and recall your nonnegotiable allegiance to fairness and fidelity. An impulse to insult or argue may be nullified by bringing up your pact with yourself to solve problems without aggression.

We discussed in the last chapter how you can keep your momentum going when you're running out of steam and can't take a time-out. By learning how to manage your energy, a priceless skill not many professionals are even aware of, you are able to sustain yourself in situations that might topple less evolved attorneys. Now, by getting clear on what matters most to you and relying on that for unwavering strength and support, you will get to a whole new level of sure-footed endurance. As we reach the end of the book, that endurance is what will keep you on the right track when you finish the next chapter and begin to lawyer like an athlete on your own.

If you're sensing a values inventory coming up at some point, you are right. But before we get into that, I want to round out the values concept a bit more and get specific about why intimately knowing and taking cues from your values is so powerful.

First, think about values like this:

Imagine you are driving your car to a place you've never been. When you plug that destination into your GPS, you are provided with directions programmed to get you to your endpoint most efficiently from where you are now. Keeping your destination in mind helps you to stay committed and hopeful as you encounter detours, traffic jams, poor weather conditions, and other challenges along the way. Lose sight of your destination and get distracted, and you are more likely to make a mistake, lose your impetus, stay where you are, go backwards, or arrive at the wrong place.

You're already seeing, as you become habituated to the work-plus model, that you are more likely to get to your destination of exquisite self-care, grounded perspective, healthy relationships, and nourishing diversions by following the prescribed steps of an expert. You are even more likely to embrace that work-plus model when you recognize that what you are really working toward is what you have come to see as the bedrock to your personal and professional fulfillment: physical and mental health. Because you deem your physical and mental health as prizes that will bring you the most satisfaction, you are now increasingly asking yourself as you move through life and work:

Will that action get in the way of or get me closer to the physical and mental health necessary to lawyer like an athlete?

> "When you operate from your values, recognizing what you want above all else, you have a straighter, simpler route to your endpoint."

When you operate from your values, recognizing what you want above all else, you have a straighter, simpler route to your endpoint. Valuing your physical and mental health will make the choice obvious when you are trying to decide things like should I order dessert? Should I take a break? Should I buy a bigger size or exercise more? Should I spend my time internet surfing or call my best friend?

You get the drill already, see? Now I want you to take a deeper look within to pinpoint other values you can look to for direction, motivation, and focus.

Now, here's that inventory you've been expecting, to help you get clearer on what really matters to you so you can operate from that more heartening place.

Attorney in Action

Eliza, an experienced attorney in the military, came for coaching because the everyday work of being an attorney was boring compared to law school. She realized through our talks that law school had been far more interesting because the prospect of applying all the learning to helping people was exciting to her. She had become so mired in minutiae since passing the bar that she wasn't experiencing any sense of usefulness to others. Eliza realized she could be more stimulated as an attorney by reminding herself that even though she wasn't seeing big results all the time, she was still making a difference. I advised printing out emails from occasionally grateful clients and keeping them in a "clients I've helped" folder so she could see evidence of her progress anytime she was losing faith. I also recommended more in-person meetings with clients so that she could feel good about being a supportive listener during dehumanizing bureaucratic procedures. Just by making these small changes, Eliza felt a resurgence of that law school excitement.

List what you are most proud of in your life:

____

____

____

Imagine you overhear your colleagues/friends describing you positively. Write down what they are saying.

____

____

____

Think about a current challenge in your life. Imagine that it's one year from now and you're listening to your kids or a mentor describing how you handled this challenge. Write down what you want them to be saying:

____

____

____

Picture yourself five years from now being honored for a noteworthy contribution you have made. Who is honoring you and what for?

____

____

____

Envision yourself nearing retirement age, whatever that age is for you. List three thing you want to have accomplished:

1. ____
2. ____
3. ____

Imagine being given $1 million . . . what would you do with that windfall?

____

____

____

Attorney in Action

Miller came for coaching because he'd been offered a big promotion at his firm but wasn't sure if he wanted to take it, though the money and perks were incredible. He'd learned during his tenure there so far that his firm put getting work done fast before thorough proofing. He was going back and forth between money and reputation, which was causing him anxiety. When he took the time to talk through his feelings, Miller realized that professional excellence was more important to him than financial security and turned down the promotion. Though it was hard to forgo a big raise, he felt the more enduring kind of stability and security associated with taking value-driven risks. With a greater sense of self-respect, he started looking for a firm that shared his dedication to quality over speed.

As with past chapters, what you have when you complete an inventory like this is a blueprint of sorts from which to build. In this case, you have a clearer idea of the values you want leading you.

Go over your inventory answers, and write the values that jump out to you below. You may have listed being debt-free, sober, or a good parent as things you are proud of, so maintaining this status quo is likely important to you. Perhaps you said you'd like to catch your colleagues saying you're reasonable, flexible, and easy to be around, so striving to behave in these ways is smart for you. You get the idea:

____

____

____

> "It's important to consider that because values are often abstract concepts, they must be brought down to earth and reinforced in your everyday life."

Now that you've identified the values you want guiding you, it's important to consider that because values are often abstract concepts, they must be brought down to earth and reinforced in your everyday life. You can keep your values present and powerful in these ways:

Regularly review your values: Look at the facts of your existence squarely, and be frank with yourself about where you might be contradicting your values. If you say you value people and relationships, are you making time for them? If you say you value the natural world, are you doing all you can to help the environment? If you say you value trustworthiness, are you being as sincere as you could be? Upholding your values tends to require uncommon determination, bravery, and humility, so there will always be room for growth here.

Look at any recent credit card statements, and note any discrepancies between your values and how you are spending your money. For example, you might say you value learning, and yet you are paying to stream shows that dull your brain; you might say you value simple living, and yet you are eating out at expensive restaurants more than feels right to you.

List some ways you could be more in alignment with your values at home:

____

____

____

Now list some ways you could be more in alignment with your values at work:

____

____

____

Keep your values close at hand: It's astonishingly easy for the undertow of immediate cravings, urges, and temper to obscure your view of even your most essential values. So, it's important to keep your values right where you can see them in the environments you're in the most. This might mean putting a picture of your kids on your desk to remind you that they are worth getting through a particularly trying workday. It could also mean posting a photo of your ideal retirement home on your fridge to remind you why you're working so hard.

One way you can make your values more prominent in your life:

____

____

____

Know that values change over time: Recall a few things you valued 10, 15, and 20 years ago. Probably a different list from what you value now, right? Part of that is maturity; popularity is a common value for teens, for example, but self-confident adults value personal preference over doing what is "cool" or "trendy." Another part is our snowballing access to information that gives us more and more ideas for things we want to do, places we want to go, what we want to have, and who we want to be. Also, unexpected circumstances can change our values abruptly; a serious diagnosis could suddenly make getting better your top value; news of an impending layoff may in an instant make financial security your most important goal.

List any long-held values that may no longer be true for you:

____

____

____

Attorney in Action

Kannika came to therapy because she'd gotten what she'd been longing for: a job that involved international travel. After years of applying for the right opportunity, she was inexplicably surprised by her lackadaisical response. How could a goal she'd been passionate about now not seem to matter? She discovered through our talks that travel, a value she'd held dear when she'd started out as a single attorney in her 30s, wasn't so enthralling as a married attorney in her 40s with aging parents living nearby. Now her primary value was being close to her parents to enjoy the time they had left; though Kannika still valued travel, she felt at this settled stage of life that she wanted to travel with her husband on vacation and not be away from family for work.

List any emerging value that may be calling you:

____

____

____

Living from your values is in no way reflexive, especially if your values are in the interest of bucking convention in the law and the greater world that may conflict with them. However, the confidence, lucidity, and peace of mind that comes from letting your values take the lead will steadily ground you amid opposition. Once you feel more comfortably immersed in the stream of your values, you can move on to the final chapter for some pivotal parting counsel.

14

Go the Distance

You've probably been here before. Eager as you enter the final chapter of a self-enrichment book, certain that you'll follow all of the way through with the wisdom you've gained from it. In this case, you now know everything you need to know to accomplish what's most important to you, and you are ready to advance assertively with that purpose.

Nothing will stop you. Not a chance. You can't go wrong.

Until the unthinkable happens, that is.

Until life gets in the way.

Life getting in the way might look like:

- Ted Williams, one of the greatest baseball hitters of all time, can no longer ignore his inner voice telling him to take a break from his sport to serve his country in World War II.
- Olympic sprinter and hurdler Gail Devers gets diagnosed out of nowhere with a debilitating autoimmune disorder.
- Yankees pitcher CC Sabathia has the epiphany that he must retreat from baseball and address his alcoholism if he wants to stay in top form and relevant.
- Superbowl-winning quarterback Peyton Manning misses an entire season from a herniated disc.
- Golf icon Tiger Woods's disturbing domestic problems become international news literally overnight.
- Champion obstacle course racer Amelia Boone decides she can no longer ignore her eating disorder and takes a leave of absence to get help.

Just like star athletes, attorneys need to not only excel at whole-person self-care, relationships, and attitude to succeed; they also must be able to deal with impediments swiftly. The awareness and agility it takes to live and work at a higher level than most must also encompass dealing with setbacks positively and proactively lest they cause undue disruption. These sports examples I've cited are dramatic, but they all bring home the essential caveat: there is no telling what lies ahead, but complications certainly will occur.

Because no matter how galvanizing this book has been for you, no matter how devoted you are to applying the work-plus model, no matter how practiced you are at putting the principles into action, you will go only so far down your lawyer-like-an-athlete path before something will knock you off track. Maybe a devastating breakup will leave you in the dust. Perhaps a horrible new boss will shake your resolve, or a family crisis could hit you at your core. Hopefully, it won't be a life-altering event that gets between you and your goals. More likely it will be a plain, old-fashioned bad day—or string of bad days—that will pull you off even your strictest, most carefully secured course.

Before I go on, I want to be very clear that the last thing I want to do is dampen your enthusiasm. I just want to temper what psychologists call "self-help euphoria," that tendency to become so positive about possibility that you haven't accounted for the opposing force of everyday existence outside the motivational experience. Unless you have pragmatic footing under the hype, your newfound resolve will quickly dissipate.

> "No matter how galvanizing this book has been for you, no matter how devoted you are to applying the work-plus model, no matter how practiced you are at putting the principles into action, you will go only so far down your lawyer-like-an-athlete path before something will knock you off track."

You can prolong your momentum by preparing to prevail when the real world throws you curveballs. You have a lot to celebrate, and I want you to do that very soon. However, make sure to protect your trajectory by heeding my advice.

You can expect to fall off the wagon occasionally when you move on from this book. Even if you've applied my strategies so rigorously that you consider yourself a bona fide

> "Even if you've applied my strategies so rigorously that you consider yourself a bona fide lawyer-like-an-athlete pro, your plans will definitely be disrupted because, well, life is just like that."

lawyer-like-an-athlete pro, your plans will definitely be disrupted because, well, life is just like that. You're feeling more on top of things, less encumbered, and moving at an agreeable pace, and it's great that you're not unduly dwelling on inner critical talk or feedback from others. That said, you are mortal, and so it follows that unfortunate, inconvenient, and seemingly unmanageable things will still jostle you. As you've moved through one chapter building on another, you've witnessed how reaching a new place in your evolution can attract additional tests and struggles that will spur further growth. That trend is part of the human condition, especially when you are ambitious and not willing to settle for the ordinary.

Of course, the advanced well-being you're cultivating isn't possible without continued risk-taking and nurturing, and not meeting the challenges of that evolution will stall you. So, please consider the following pointers for efficiently weathering any possible storms ahead:

Make sure you have support: Because much of what you've learned from this book is not standard for most attorneys, you may regress a bit if you don't have meaningful others in your life who practice the work-plus model too. So, seek out attorneys who, whether they've read this book or not, get the commitment and diligence it takes to fully embrace my philosophy. You understand the importance of positive social experiences in your life, and keeping company with those whose values resonate most with you. Steer clear of others who resist or devalue your enlightened approach. If you know other attorneys who have read the book and want to stick with it, stay in regular touch with them so that you can commiserate around the ups and downs you experience. Maybe start a book group and work on the program with colleagues to keep it going, or do a presentation for a committee you're on, talk about it with your boss, or write about it for your state bar journal. The physical and mental action of discussing and teaching the book will reinforce the synapses in your brain into finer and finer shape.

Be patient with the more stubborn challenges: Though you have learned to feel more in charge and fulfilled by adopting more productive habits, there will always be times when entrenched beliefs pull you back into old ways of operating. Maintain a healthy respect for the daunting fallacies that make lawyering so unnecessarily hard, such as:

- You will end up on the street if you ever turn away a client.
- Recreation and replenishment are the antithesis of productivity rather than the bedrock of it.
- You must come across as tough, unflappable, and never wrong to be respected.
- Enforcing boundaries and limits with clients and telling them the unvarnished truth will just drive them away.
- Vacations obstruct rather than increase billable hours.
- Resilience is about pushing through, fueling yourself with fast-acting stimulants, then crashing.

Yes, you've unmasked these fear-inducing convictions for the oppressive myths they are, but they run deep and rear up when you're not looking. So, be especially gentle with yourself as you chip away at them.

Beware of wake-up calls: You may remember me telling you at the start of this book that you might discover along the way that some big, intimidating life changes could ultimately be in order. As my coaching clients become more attuned to themselves through my strategies, they often have realizations from their growth that lead to difficult decisions and problems. As you become more aligned with new goals and conditions, you may outgrow people, places, and things you never thought you'd outgrow. As you improve your habits and perspective, it may hit you that you need to uproot yourself from a significant relationship, job, homestead, or habit. Making alterations integral to your continued growth and development will bring you to

> "Making alterations integral to your continued growth and development will bring you to increasingly more agreeable circumstances and contexts than you may imagine."

Attorney in Action

Audrey had come to coaching two years before to position herself for her vocational dream: a seat on her state bench. She was so close, in the midst of final interviews, she could practically touch it, and she was ready. Then, inexplicably, as if a rug were being pulled from under her, she lost to someone less experienced, leaving her with the sense she'd been unfairly overlooked. After processing her considerable anger and disappointment, Audrey saw a silver lining: she'd been striving so hard to be on that bench that she'd overlooked opportunities right there at her firm that were actually more aligned with the values she had evolved since starting her quest for the bench. To her surprise, she wound up being grateful for the loss because she ended up gaining so much more.

increasingly more agreeable circumstances and contexts than you may imagine. Still, transition is rough, so make sure to process your emotions around it, take extra good care of yourself during periods of upheaval, and get guidance and bolstering as you reorganize.

Honor internal disruptions: You've learned by now to listen to yourself and act on your surest and truest inner inclinations. Doing that when you're being supported by a steadying, centering book is one thing, but persisting amid the clamor and confusion of modern life is quite another. To persevere as you lawyer like an athlete, you must very conscientiously be open to acknowledging interior cues needed to stay on course. If you've been faithfully working out three times a week and suddenly you want to go back to sleep rather than hit the gym, recognize that you are doing too much of a good thing and need some rest. If after weeks of thinking more innovatively at work, you're feeling inexplicably uninspired and blocked, take a breather to continue your roll.

If you have a growing inkling about something in your life that may no longer be right, do some experimentation around that, and see if some tweaks alone can correct your course. If you're feeling the stirrings of sickness, put aside whatever you're doing, get some rest, and come back when your symptoms are gone. You're well aware that ignoring messages from within to push through work is pretty much

> "You're well aware that ignoring messages from within to push through work is pretty much the essence of the attorney stress problem, and heeding those messages as they emerge makes for much less chaos than waiting for them to get unwieldy."

the essence of the attorney stress problem, and heeding those messages as they emerge makes for much less chaos than waiting for them to get unwieldy. Remember that if you're feeling anxiety beyond what it takes to motivate you and running into resistance, you should evaluate your goals to make sure they're still resonant with your values and energy level, that your tiny steps are tiny enough, and that you're rewarding yourself sufficiently.

Honor external disruptions: For the most part, you've learned not to be unnecessarily fazed by circumstances beyond your control. However, even with the more grounded composure you have gained, some uncontrollable factors around you will still have the potential to sap the energy you need to lawyer like an athlete. For example, a layoff, family member in peril, serious character attack, or your computer crashing could come out of nowhere and

Attorney in Action

Margot sought coaching to progress at an extremely demanding firm not at all open to the work-plus model. The more she grew from our sessions, the more blocked and frustrated she felt. The last thing she wanted to do was job-hunt, especially because she valued the financial security her firm offered, but her intuition was telling her that she had to accept that her workplace was toxic, and she had to get out. It wasn't easy to get psyched up for this because she didn't have faith that there was anything better out there for her. By exploring despite her skepticism, Margot gradually learned that progressive firms did exist, and soon she got an offer—considerably more than she was making, with better benefits—from one of them. By facing the fear and imposition of finding a supportive work environment, she put herself in a position to thrive in a way that would never have been possible at her former job.

leave you reeling, and you might cope with that added stress by eating too much junk food, letting clutter gather around you, or having a major meltdown—after all, you are human. Athletes step out occasionally to recover from an injury or personal setback, and they often come back in better shape than before. By putting themselves first, they prioritize what matters as they acclimate to their new reality. Likewise, you will get back to your better ways if you take time to regroup when outside triggers pull you away, and your work, reputation, and smarter habits will still be there when you bounce back. However, you'll only sabotage your success by pushing to accomplish "it all" when "it all" suddenly snowballs.

Appreciate that the work-plus plan is continuous—and contagious: Because there is no such thing as perfection, there is no such thing as a perfect match between the work-plus model on paper and the actual attorneys practicing it. Look at the model one more time below, and remember to use it as a compass for orientation and direction, not as a destination to be replicated exactly:

Attorney in Action

Hans was really getting this book down, and the positive changes he was seeing in himself were making him increasingly interested in advancing the work-plus model. Because he was working more efficiently, he had time to take acting classes, something he'd been wanting to do for a long time. He was considering auditioning for a community theater production when his son began having troubling behavioral issues at school. Hans realized from tossing and turning at night and resuming some unproductive habits that he couldn't pursue his acting passion and help his son simultaneously, so he decided to make his son the priority for as long as necessary. Several months later, when his son was doing better thanks to Hans's extra attention, Hans got back to his thespian sideline.

Don't assume the work-plus model is fixed since life is filled with fluctuations. So, just when you think you have it totally down, something will happen to remind you that noticing, assessing, shifting, and readjusting will always be part of the lawyer-like-an-athlete commitment. You may be really happy with your social life and a relationship inexplicably dissolves; you may finally consider yourself an optimist and your mood takes a major nosedive; and on and on it goes with your work-plus components needing adjustment. There will always be some part of the model requiring your attention, often more than one at a time, but that's just the dance of your inner and outer worlds that you're always going to have to tango with. The upside is that when you breathe new life into whatever work-plus component needs revision, it will energize other components.

"There will always be some part of the model requiring your attention, often more than one at a time, but that's just the dance of your inner and outer worlds that you're always going to have to tango with."

Attorney in Action

Tax attorney Natasha had reached a juncture with me months ago where she didn't need regular coaching sessions anymore. She came in for a tune-up because she'd fallen into some old workaholic habits during tax season and was neglecting her self-care and relationships. True to every hardcore, ambitious person, she was frantic that if she didn't turn things around at once, everything would fall apart. Since she already knew the tiny-step method, it wasn't hard for her to see that regrouping would amount to starting with a manageable plan. Because she was most stressed by guilt over not doing her part in her relationships, we began with these simple goals: sending an overdue birthday card, setting up a coffee date, and texting her closest friend. By helping Natasha to feel more connected and calmer, these initial movements led to improvements with self-care, such as eating breakfast more often and going to the dentist. Pretty soon Natasha was back where she wanted to be, with greater confidence in her capacity to recalibrate.

Do it just for today: I'm not a substance-abuse expert, and while I value many recovery options, I firmly believe that Alcoholics Anonymous has the best advice out there for lifestyle change: *take it one day at a time*. If you think right now that you're going to practice your new habits for the rest of your life, the prospect can seem exhausting. You're much more likely to stay in this for the long haul if you focus on making the most of the day you are in. Wake up with the intention to lawyer like an athlete as best you can, knowing that you will make mistakes and not always feel like doing those things you know you should be doing. Ask yourself at the end of each day what went wrong, what you can let go of, and what new discoveries you can wake up with as you greet the fresh slate of a new day.

Most of all, be easy on yourself: Infusing your work performance with exquisite self-care, a grounded perspective, healthy relationships, and nourishing diversions is the solution to the attorney stress problem, but practicing all this is something that the establishment hasn't fully embraced and is reluctant to buy into.

Attorney in Action

My client Joe, hard of hearing his whole life, obviously has more challenges than most attorneys. He has had to learn to function in a hearing world, adapting himself to catch up and get along, often dealing with people who equate not hearing with not being competent. He gets through most days just fine, but there are times when practicing the work-plus model while also navigating his disability just feels like too much. Joe has learned on those days to drop anything that can wait, modify his expectations, put tomorrow out of his mind, and do only what he absolutely must do now. Because he is experienced at giving himself compassion and grace, and letting go when he needs to, he sees that he is "on" more than he is "off," and that ascending trend of overall consistency pulls him forward.

As long as the convention is to work incessantly without regard for the destructive consequences of that, you are not just an attorney aiming to be more successful; you are a brave pioneer on a whole new frontier.

When you're inclined to give up because it's just too damn hard, take stock of the fact that what really makes athletes most triumphant is not just success with their sport but their insistence on valuing their personal health and safety over financial gain and glory. The professional sports world was once just as dysfunctional and punishing as the law world, not seeing how elemental a full-bodied life is to full-bodied performance. The professional sports world is getting smarter because exceptionally daring athletes like Simone Biles, who dropped out two years ago to take care of herself then dazzled us with her recent comeback, are defying and disrupting an abusive system to compete on their terms. Most important,

"When you're inclined to give up because it's just too damn hard, take stock of the fact that what really makes athletes most triumphant is not just success with their sport but their insistence on valuing their personal health and safety over financial gain and glory."

people on every side of sports are seeing that these new terms are a win-win for all.

The pressure to work past the point of what's healthy isn't totally going away—in sports or law—anytime soon. You, much like those unconventional individual athletes who don't go along with popular but absurd rules, will be most powerful when you operate from your own version of success. You're equipped with the playbook for that, and so it's a matter of always remembering to carve a new pathway; it isn't easy but it's beyond worth it. This won't ever be smooth sailing, but the more you persist, the more you will be in a position of positive influence, and the less opposition you will face. The wondrous vibe you'll exude from that will have the magnetic effect of encouraging and engaging others.

You know from all my client examples that there are already many informed attorneys out there, and you are probably feeling an increased sense of company. Attorneys are especially objective people who will try new things once they see the logic of them, and that, of course, is what drives transformation. What I'm teaching is catching on because attorneys are seeing from their own experimentation that it really works.

You've probably noticed growing continuing legal education (CLE) opportunities for being more psychologically fit, and I see in my own work an increase in attorneys and organizations wanting support for their well-being. I also see attorneys being more willing to take time away from work to get coaching. Recently, believe it or not, the head of a firm paid me to convince a partner to take a vacation, and I was just asked to do a talk for new attorneys on the importance of in-person interaction. Yes, it's still hard to imagine getting out from under the schedule of the courts, but I do believe the tables are turning toward attorneys.

It's clear that there's a real movement happening, and you are part of it. That's a pretty exciting note for us to end on. You can keep that excitement going by staying connected with what *you're* excited about.

> "You have a spellbinding power to feel in control in an out-of-control world."

You have a spellbinding power to feel in control in an out-of-control world. Your happiness comes from giving yourself space to grow; you understand the real

Attorney in Action: YOU

Having given their all to incorporating the principles, [Fill your name in here] had felt certain when they closed the cover of *Lawyer Like an Athlete* two months ago that they were completely set up for success. Now, out of the everyday guidance and structure that book provided, they are seeing that they're slipping back into their old ways and they wonder: *Did I read the wrong book? Is there a better system I should try? Was I crazy to think I could actually do this?* Fortunately, they are less reactive than they used to be, so they stop for a moment, take some deep breaths, and refocus on the reality that they're not back to square one; this is a nonlinear, ever-evolving process that they've been trained to steer through. Then they ask the crucial question—*What tiny step will get me back into the lawyer-like-an-athlete-game?*—and they realize *I have what I need to take it from here.*

victory is not in getting an insane amount of work done but in actualizing a more sensible and satisfying metric for achievement.

If you keep at this, you'll add to the momentum of replacing stress with your own definition of success. So, go forth unapologetically in the words of Sha'Carri Richardson, the fastest track and fielder alive who has made and recovered from some embarrassing public mistakes: "I'm not worried about the world anymore. I've seen the world be my friend; I've seen the world turn on me. At the end of the day, I've always been with me."[1]

The more you're with you, the easier this gets.

Stay tuned in with yourself. Keep asking what needs your attention, what modification might smooth your way. Go about that with the same curiosity that got you to pick up and stay with this book. Don't feel the need to quantify it; give yourself permission to do what feels right whenever possible. Most of all, remember, you have everything it takes to feel like you're reigning over your work and life instead of getting consumed by it.

---

[1] Muskan Sharma, "Never Allow the Media, Never Allow Outsiders, Never Allow Anything but Yourself To Define Who You Are," Sportskeeda, August 23, 2023, https://www.sportskeeda.com/athletics/news-never-allow-media-never-allow-outsiders-never-allow-anything-define-are-sha-carri-richardson.

ACKNOWLEDGMENTS

This book would not have happened without the support and skills of many people. First and foremost, I want to thank Heidi K. Brown for so generously connecting me, a virtual stranger, with her contact at the American Bar Association. I extend deep gratitude to my writing coach, Mark Chimsky, and my editor, Lorraine Murray, for being honest with their feedback and making me a better author. A very special shout-out goes to my husband, Mike Coughlan, whose sports knowledge and eagle eye improved every chapter. Most important, I want to thank Mike and my cherished family members, friends, and colleagues (the list is long and you know who you are!) for giving me the space, encouragement, and levity that propelled me toward the finish line.

INDEX